To Gulliver,

No creatures abject
you have!

Praise for
The QUIT Alternative

"Most people who are unhappy at work think that the only alternative is to escape, which sometimes leads to risky situations. Ben Fanning proves, with real-life stories, practical advice, and tested methods, that you can completely change how you feel and perform at work by taking the driver's seat in your career. This should be required reading for all employees."
–Pamela Slim, **author of** *Body of Work*

"Ben hits the nail on the head. It's about taking ownership, about knowing what we want, what we stand for and bringing it! He addresses how self awareness and attitude can give us the power to shape our jobs and our career."
–Hans Hickler, **former CEO of DHL and founder of Ellipsis Advisors**

"The QUIT Alternative is real world experience written by the Zen Master of Career/Stress Management. Having worked with Ben and followed his practice, this book is a great study for anyone looking to merge their work/life balance while continuing to advance career goals."
–Mark Albright, **Vice President at Sports Authority**

"A unique and healthy approach to managing your career and life. In a world of job-hopping to get ahead, Ben provides a good mix of advice and life experiences for those who feel the grass is always greener."
–Brandy Maranian, **Senior Vice President at CareFusion and former VP of KRAFT Foods**

THE
QUIT
ALTERNATIVE

The Blueprint for Creating the job You Love WITHOUT Quitting

BEN FANNING

To my family, clients, coworkers,
and the next generation of employees.

ISBN: 978-1-941142-60-8

Published by JETLAUNCH
www.jetlaunch.net

Table of Contents

CHAPTER 7
CAMPAIGN FOR THE WORK
YOU LOVE
75

You have the power to get more of the work you love. Stop advertising that you're happy doing work you hate. 7 steps to inspiring work. Planting seeds with your boss. 10 strategies to boost your reputation and become an expert.

SECTION III
CREATE AND SUSTAIN THE JOB YOU LOVE

CHAPTER 8
NEGOTIATE—WITHOUT OTHERS LOSING
89

The awkward experience that taught me everything is negotiable. Negotiate for yourself without disrespecting anyone. Relocating to the city of your dreams without having to quit. 6 ways to say "no" without getting fired. Dealing with an unreasonable boss. Creating the win-win-win.

CHAPTER 9
OWN YOUR MESSAGE
107

Market to your boss and coworkers. The email headline that always gets a response. A simple question that reduces anxiety. "How can I more effectively get my message across?" Lead with WIFM. Prioritize the call to action. Paying for your MBA with OPM.

CHAPTER 10
BRING YOUR PERSONAL SIDE TO WORK
115

How to bring yourself to the office. Energized and authentic. Warning: this might be fun. Blurring the lines between the personal and professional. The "How was Your Weekend" Test.

Companion resources
for this book:
benfanning.com/quit

The Game You Most Want to Win

Ben and I are friends, and we are working on some of the same things, including how to own the game you most want to win. We both want you to take ownership of your choices and to move decisively in a direction that you choose, versus how lots of people do things, which is to see what happens and then react. But I tend to put a lot of my emphasis on how to go off and run your own business, and Ben believes while you could choose that option, you might have a perfectly good job that doesn't need quitting. And I think Ben's smart for this.

Running a company is difficult. It sounds thrilling, until you realize that it makes you the head of sales. It might seem like being the boss is great, until you're the one having to figure out how to keep everyone on the team paid. There are many complexities that come with running your own company, and it's a safe bet that most people underestimate the amount of work that is required to tackle running your own business.

Besides, as I already said, maybe your job is great, or maybe it could be great—with a few tweaks. That's where Ben comes in. That's where this book comes in.

Games are easy to understand in most cases. There are rules, players, scoring, and strategy in all games. If I ask you to describe Tic Tac Toe, you could do so easily. Now, if I ask you to describe the strategy of a parent playing Tic Tac Toe with their kid while waiting for their food to come at a restaurant, the strategy part of the game changes dramatically. Right?

What Ben has done for you in this book is that he's shown you how your job might have fairly simple or assumed rules, scores, players, and strategy, but that maybe there's more than one strategy and maybe there are different games that overlay the one you think is the important one, and that maybe, with a little bit of learning, you'll be able to do something truly great with your effort. Heck, Ben Fanning shows you that every one of those variables is in play. He uses different words than I do, but the premise is very much there. You can win, especially if you rethink how you're playing.

Pay close attention. Books like this aren't something you read and then discard. There's work to be done here. You have to take action. You have to practice. You have to plan. But with that, you'll have a shot at owning the game known as your job. And once you own it? You'll have a shot at winning. And we all love to win.

—Chris Brogan, **CEO Owner Media Group, and New York Times bestselling author of** *The Freaks Shall Inherit the Earth*

The QUIT Alternative

Everyone Saves When You Create the Job You Love Instead of Quitting

COST TO CEOS

87% of employees aren't fully engaged at work

Rehiring and Retraining

$61,500 per employee

Disengaged employees are 2.5 times more likely to quit.

Lost Productivity

$7,857 per employee

COST TO EMPLOYEES

BREAKDOWN

The cost of starting a new job adds up quickly

The money you save by staying at your current job could buy a new car

UP TO

$36,573

Cost of Your Time	Loss of Vacation Time	No Promotion or Raises	Stress from Starting a New Job
$15,000	$12,000	$6,090	$3,483

Resources: Gallup, US Bureau Labor and Stats, Dale Carnagie, About.com, MIT Sloan Mgt Review, CNN, Holmes and Rahe Stress Scale

CONTROL YOUR DESTINY

Here's an empowering perspective that puts you in the driver's seat of your career and allows you to take control of your destiny—Create the job you love.

When you adopt this perspective, you discover that long-term success doesn't necessarily come from winning that promotion, acing the interview, networking with the right people, or even being in the right place at the right time.

Success more reliably comes from engaging with the full potential of your current job, marshaling the resources around you, and seizing the opportunities that are there for the taking.

This idea will ignite your career just as it has ignited my career and the careers of many of my clients.

But there's an even bigger picture here.

Creating the job you love is an exhilarating and invigorating way to live. It calls upon your personal strengths and taps into your internal motivation.

It's a job and a way of life created on the foundation of the authentic you. You will feel more alive than ever before.

Sounding good? Read on.

The One Word that Will Ignite Your Career

Not only will one word ignite your career, it can completely transform your life.

This occurs when you shift your professional quest from "*finding* the job you love"—

"To **creating** the job you love."

Simply substitute "create" for "find."

Easy, right?

But consider that most people never adopt this perspective. How many times have you heard someone talk about "finding a job?"

Maybe they continue the search to find the perfect job for an entire life time or maybe somewhere along the line they give up all together.

"Finding" becomes a distraction.

It's an anemic perspective. The roots of its weakness come from the very definition of the word, "Find: to discover or perceive by chance or unexpectedly."

By changing this word to "create," you shift perspective.

"Creating" is far more powerful and is defined as "to bring something into existence." In ancient times, the word frequently appears in conjunction with the concept *creatio ex nihilo*, meaning "creation out of nothing."

Would you prefer to leave the job you love up to chance?

Or bring something you love and desire into existence *with intention*?

If this idea of intentionally creating something powerful for yourself piques your interest, then you're in the right place.

Create the Job You Love WITHOUT QUITTING

One of the guiding principles of this book is that you can create the job you love without having to quit your current job.

Most people are relieved by this idea.

Imagine a work day in which you're engaged, performing with maximum impact, and playing in the "sweet spot."

> My premise is that most people are better off investing in their current job by securing more work that inspires them.

What if you could achieve all this while you remain in your current job—and keep the steady paycheck, 401(k), and insurance?

Sounds pretty good, right?

But if you're like most people I meet, at some point along the way you'll find your day crammed full of work you're required to do but don't enjoy. Frustration follows, then resentment. If it continues too long you may disengage, maybe begin looking for a new job or fantasizing about "passive income."

Maybe you're feeling that you've grown as much as you can in your current position, and you're not sure what to do next.

Maybe you have an inkling of what you like most about your current job, but you're not sure how this translates into your next step within your company.

Perhaps you're feeling a little discouraged with how your career is turning out, and you feel powerless to control your own destiny at work.

Or you could be feeling that no matter what you do, it won't work out.

If any of these scenarios apply, don't worry. The good news is that you can start from wherever you are right now in your career.

> This book guides you through, starting with your current job with all its imperfections and challenges, and turning these into opportunities to bring out your personal best.

The Real Work of Your Career

Remember the excitement as you neared graduation day of finding the job you'd love?

Maybe you had a burning desire for the corner office and a dream of jet-setting around the world as an executive of a large organization. Oh, the prestige and the impact on the world—and, boy, wouldn't the parents be proud!

Looking back, everyone was talking about *finding the job* but no one was having the conversation about *creating one*. Finding a job requires you to fit yourself into a job that someone else has created.

The common perspective is that you should fit yourself into that dream job, whether or not it's a good fit. Not succeeding in that endeavor could mean unemployment or even worse, humiliation. So most people master the skills of interviewing, selling themselves, and networking to ensure that won't happen.

Maybe you sped towards a career path, yet never considered creating the right job to fit your passion, capabilities, and the needs of an organization.

> "Creating the job you love" is choosing to make your job something worth fully investing yourself in.

If you've ever uttered the phrase, "finding the job," then you've operated on this limiting belief too. Once upon a time, I believed that the job I could love and the path to the corner office were out there waiting if I just kept searching.

Under this false pretense, I propelled myself through four companies in four cities, making each move because the next best thing was too good to pass up.

But I missed something along the way, and I'll share with you in this book how I discovered the path to changing my work day without quitting the job I had.

Your Mission—to Create the Job the You Love

Instead of fantasizing about finding the perfect job, you can get on a mission to create a job you will love.

It changes everything when you raise your eyes from the treadmill and begin to approach your work day like a leader. You begin to work on your terms and find new sparks of possibility that maybe you failed to see before. These sparks may grow into a steady and sustaining fire.

The message I'd send you (and myself) back in college as graduation day neared:

> *Dear Graduate,*
>
> *The job you love doesn't exist. The real work is to create the job you love.*
>
> *Yours truly,*
> *Ben*

It took me a decade out of college to grasp this message.

Where We're Headed Together

Instead of quitting or fantasizing about leaving a job, we're going to invest your time, energy, and resources into transforming the job you have.

Here's an overview of my personal playbook for creating a job you will love in three steps that you can begin to act on today.

Each of this book's three sections covers one step and includes practical strategies to create the job you will love no matter where you are in your career.

Step 1: Engage with the Potential of Your Current Job

Choose a more empowering alternative to the "stay or leave" question by engaging with the potential of your current job. Do this by redefining your beliefs about work and giving yourself permission to love your work. Then turn your work into something you can look forward to by choosing to look in new ways at your job and even those meetings you dread.

Step 2: Cultivate Work that Inspires You

A job you love is full of work that motivates you. It doesn't mean the work is easy, but it does mean that you find yourself more enthusiastic and excited to walk in through the office door on Monday mornings. I'll share practical strategies to discover and campaign for this inspiring work and protect yourself against an overload of the work you don't like. Then we'll wrap up with how you can build momentum to carry you through even the toughest days.

Step 3: Create and Sustain the Job You Love

Once you're on the way to creating the job you love, it's important to learn the skills to sustain it. You'll discover how to negotiate on your own behalf without harm to your boss or coworkers and begin to bring a negotiation perspective to work every day. I'll also share how to own the outcome of your messages so they're heard and compel others to action. You'll then learn how to reap the benefits of sharing your personal side at work. We'll conclude with ways to turn your office into a more inspiring place to work.

It's time to create the job you will love.

So let's get going!
Ben

Note: Companion resources available at benfanning.com/quit

SECTION I

Engage With the Potential of Your Current Job

S ection I begins with the wake-up call that led me to see the dead end I was headed for.

You might be surprised by how personal I get here, but I want to show you the full consequences of the "finding a job" spiral. Section I then moves into the first steps to take to discover the amazing possibilities that open up when you start looking for work that inspires you.

Enjoy!

Chapter 1

THE WAKE-UP CALL

*Your work is going to fill a large part of your life, and the only way
to be truly satisfied is to do what you believe is great work. And the
only way to do great work is to love what you do.*

Steve Jobs, Stanford Commencement Address, 2005

woke up sweating in the middle of the night with the weight of a
bowling ball on my chest.

I'd had a premonition of having a heart attack one day because of
my family history of heart attacks, as well as high daily stress, but I
never imagined it would happen in my 30s!

Can't Get No Satisfaction

Working harder than ever, I wasn't satisfied with the title, the
paycheck, or the life. Never being satisfied was okay with me
because it kept me striving.

The crisis came when I relocated to Manhattan and permanent
uneasiness set in. A gnawing feeling replaced what had once felt
like ambition. The gnawing intensified as an 80-hour work week
became my norm, not including the 3-hour round-trip daily
commute.

Every time I walked in the office door, my jaw clenched.

The Physical Impact

I brought the stress home. I began grinding my teeth at night so loudly that it kept my wife awake. I developed a small pop when I chewed. I went to see a jaw specialist who offered a $1,700 custom retainer. Instead, I opted to purchase a $17 football mouth guard. The only person it helped was my wife who got a huge laugh when I wore it to bed the first night.

I felt alone. I spent more time at unhappy hour than ever before. The stress was influencing my relationship with my wife because the only conversation I could have with her concerned how much I hated my job.

I thought a getaway would help, so I scheduled a weekend at a nice resort for our anniversary.

Spa Day From Hell

Starting off our weekend with a couple's massage seemed like a great idea. We were both comfortably settled on our respective tables and enjoying the experience when Missy the Masseuse tapped me on the shoulder and whispered, "Mr. Fanning, excuse me. I just wanted to let you know that your hamstrings and quads are extremely tight, and frankly, I'm concerned. Do you stretch?" This question ruined my massage experience, and all I could answer was, "Yes, I do, but obviously not enough."

Although I thought we'd talked enough, Missy the Masseuse didn't. Thirty minutes later, she asked, "Mr. Fanning, excuse me. Do you have a shoulder injury?" I was so annoyed that I was ready to leave. She thought I hadn't heard, so she repeated her question loudly enough for my wife and the other masseuse to hear. So I simply said, "No, I do not. Why do you ask?"

Missy felt emboldened to say, "Well, your shoulders are so tight that I could not relax them one bit even after an hour. Honestly, the only parts of you that relaxed were your fingers." Embarrassed, I lay there in silence.

I was surprised (and not in a good way), but this experience brought to my attention that stress and dissatisfaction were affecting not only my personal life and relationships, but also my body in ways that I'd never imagined possible. I even developed a crease down my forehead from furrowing my brow—a scar that I still carry today.

The Story I'd Never Told

I'd never shared the next part of this story with anyone, including my wife. When she read this book in draft, she was stunned.

Let's go back to that night when I woke up with the bowling ball on my chest. My wife was out of town. I thought, "It's finally caught up with me," and hurried downstairs and hailed a cab to take me to the hospital.

On the way, I thought about calling my wife, but was too ashamed. I felt weak.

When I arrived at the ER, they rushed me back and ran some tests. Afterward, the doctor coldly entered the room and said, "Sir, you're not having a heart attack. You're having a panic attack."

When I asked what that meant, all he had for me was, "Try to relax. Learn to laugh. Talk to someone." This advice angered me.

Of course I wanted to relax! I'd been trying to relax for months— I'd taken vacations, massage, intense exercise, breathing, praying, you name it.

This terrifying wake-up call helped me recognize that I was headed for a meltdown, and something had to change.

My Wife Finally Had Enough

This is why one evening a few weeks later, when my wife slapped a list of therapists on the dinner table and told me to make the call, I didn't argue.

I also didn't make the call. Frustrated by my immense inertia, she called for me and taped a note to my bag with the appointment time and address. I was relieved.

Every week, I trudged uptown from 86th Street in Manhattan to my therapist's office. I told my boss I had a standing doctor's appointment with my wife for the next few weeks. He thought we were doing fertility treatments. I was too ashamed for anyone to know I was seeing a therapist.

What I Learned When My Shrink Fired Me

I'd vent and rant for the hour that my therapist and I sat in his dimly lit room. He'd listen and nod. One day he stopped me mid-sentence: "Ben, do you know what your problem is?" I thought, "Finally, this guy is going to earn what I'm paying. This is what I've been waiting for."

Then he said it flat out. "You're burned out and hate your job. That's not a psychiatric problem, and there's no pill for it."

I must have looked confused, because he unloaded more. "I've got sick people to deal with here. We need to end this, and you need to go work this out."

I asked, "You're firing me?" He responded, "Yes." I couldn't decide if I wanted to punch him or cry.

The Truth Hurts

I'm not recommending what this guy did as therapy. It was tough love, but he made an important point that I wasn't ready to hear.

I showed up each week with a truckload of worries and complaints. I'd walk out of his office feeling great, but within minutes of entering my own office, I'd be back in breakdown.

My sessions with him resulted in a high followed by a crash. My stress and dissatisfaction weren't resolving, and he knew it.

> I needed to take action.

The day my shrink fired me, I had a revelation. Looking back over years of big expectations, jobs, bosses, and promotions, no matter where I looked there was one common element—me.

I Decided to Stop and Listen to the Job

Nothing was wrong with my job. It was innocent, and I couldn't blame it any longer. I remember describing my job to friends who thought it sounded "really cool" and couldn't understand why I'd want to leave.

> Nothing was wrong with my job. It was innocent, and I couldn't blame it any longer.

I was in a constant state of frustration because the work I was required to spend my day doing wasn't the right fit for who I was.

But I Couldn't Quit

I saw that the problem started with me, but I didn't see that I had many options. I couldn't quit.

I had job-hopped before, and while it resulted in more money and a bigger title, it only led to the same type of frustrating work day. I fantasized about sticking it out another 20 years and retiring early, but I probably wouldn't survive that long. Plus, sacrificing my younger years for something down the road seemed ridiculous—although I'd operated under that principle for years.

I'd learned the lesson that Warren Buffet offered:

"I think you are out of your mind if you keep taking jobs that you don't like because you think it will look good on your resume. Isn't that a little like saving up sex for your old age?"

I was trapped, wearing the golden handcuffs of a bonus, 401(k), and insurance. But probably the primary trap for me was the corporate identity I'd invested so much in crafting.

Would I have to throw it all away?

Chapter 2

THE EMPOWERING ALTERNATIVE TO THE "STAY OR LEAVE" QUESTION

Whether you think you can, or think you can't—you're right.

Henry Ford, Founder of Ford Motor Company

At the end of the last chapter, I asked, "Would I have to throw it all away?"

No, and I didn't—and you don't either.

But this doesn't mean you should stay in a job that makes you feel miserable. There's a much more helpful, middle way that most people never see.

The more empowering way to handle this is to create the job you love without quitting, but before we get there, let's explore.

You see that staying in a situation that's not working for you leads to disengagement and some crazy fantasies (that I'll explore in a minute). But if you quit, you may miss out on the benefits and future opportunities of the place you are.

Disengagement, Fantasy, and the I Can't Quit Epidemic

Like so many other employees, I found myself disengaging. Miserable in my job, but convinced that quitting was impossible, I stayed at my desk but checked out mentally.

Turns out that I wasn't alone. According to Gallup, only 13% of employees are fully engaged in their work day.

> only 13% of employees are fully engaged in their work day.

The cost to companies and their people is staggering:

- **Lost Productivity?** It's estimated that disengagement costs U.S. businesses $450–550 billion in lost productivity annually. That's $6,429 per employee per year. Calculate the impact on a 10,000-person organization (7,000 of whom are disengaged), and it adds up to a startling $45 million per year.
- **Cost of Turnover?** Disengaged employees are 2.5 times more likely to quit. When you consider the costs of rehiring and retraining, this adds up to $61,500 per employee, or more than $32 million a year for a 10,000-person organization.
- **Employee Burnout?** Much more difficult to quantify but no less important is the pain suffered by individual employees and their families.

We have a generation of disconnected, burned-out employees, raising a new generation, taught to believe that all employment has to offer is pain.

The Fantasy That Destroys Careers

I was having a beer with a friend at my favorite barbecue restaurant when he started voicing his frustration with his job. He turned to me and said, "Sometimes, I just wish they'd fire me. It'd be just the kick in the ass I need to pursue a job I really love."

This was not the first time I'd heard friends who fight daily in the corporate trenches indulge in this thought. Is getting fired a legitimate path to creating the job of your dreams—or a dangerous fantasy?

Getting Fired as Fantasy

Cue the music …

Welcome to Fantasy Island, where all your "getting fired" fantasies come true.

One day the usually cheerful HR person walks into your office, all frowns, with a uniformed security guard. They strip your corporate badge (Dragnet style), drop a tiny cardboard box on your desk, and give you five minutes to pack your stuff. In your haste, you leave behind treasured corporate memorabilia, like your five-year anniversary pen and even your family photos.

You walk out in tears, past your colleagues, to the parking lot. That day you vow you'll show them.

The next week you start that pet project you've thought about for years. It quickly grows into an international behemoth corporation, and you take it public. You make the strategic decision to buy the company you used to work for. On Day One of the takeover, you stroll into your old office and publicly fire your former boss as well as that guy who wouldn't shut up in the weekly staff meetings.

After all that exhausting work, you decide to take a direct flight to Maui and sip Mai Tais by the beach and run your company remotely from there. Your day-to-day looks like the front cover of *The 4-Hour Workweek* by Tim Ferriss, including a hammock and palm trees.

Sound outstanding?

Getting Fired As Reality TV

Cue the music again …

Welcome to Real World Corporate, where people stop being polite and start getting real.

The first part of the story is the same, but it happens on a Friday afternoon in the summer when most people are away and they can fire you quietly. There are more forms to fill out before you leave, and in your stunned state, you just sign, hoping not to overlook anything important.

You leave exhilarated by the freedom but concerned about what's next, and of course, where the next paycheck will come from. You'd love to pursue one of the ideas swirling in your head, but it's overwhelming.

You don't know where to start. You're finally free, but you realize you've never worked a day without having someone set goals for you. No longer limited by annual goals or performance reviews, it's exciting to make your own rules—and even more exciting to tell other people you're making them—but the big problem is: what next?

The reality is that getting fired is devastating. Think again if you're saying, "It'd be the best thing that could happen to me."

Busting the Myth of the Four-Hour Workweek

When I burned out and dreamed of quitting, I searched Amazon for career change books. I'd read all the classics

> Fantasizing about getting fired is simply an excuse for not pursuing your dream career right where you are.

like, *What Color is Your Parachute* and *48 Days to the Job You Love*, but now I was even more frustrated and hungry for an amped up version, so I bought three books right out of the gate:

- *The 4-Hour Workweek* by Tim Ferriss
- *Career Renegade* by Jonathan Fields
- *Escape from Cubicle Nation* by Pam Slim (whose awesome other book *Body of Work* also offers some alternatives to leaving)

I read and absorbed each of these outstanding books multiple times, and they fueled my belief that I could create the job I would love—but I believed that I had to quit my current job to do so. That belief had significantly limiting consequences:

- I wasted hours day-dreaming about quitting or getting fired instead of strategizing about how to make my current job better.
- I missed out on opportunities to tackle new projects at the office that could have inspired me and expanded my skills.
- I devalued the steady paycheck that showed up in my bank account every month.
- I stopped investing in my corporate network and relationships with coworkers.
- I started to feel ashamed of my corporate background and the years I'd invested establishing my corporate identity.

> You might be better off to double down on the investment you're making in the job you have.

How Coach Nick Saban Grabbed My Attention

I once saw an interview with Alabama head football coach, Nick Saban, winner of multiple college football national championships. He's coached for a lot of teams and even had a reputation as a bit of a job hopper. He's jumped around from the NFL to college football, back to the NFL and back to college. His last stop was the University of Alabama. He's learned a lot about career development in the process.

The reporter asked about his assistant coaches who were heading to other jobs, and he responded, "Like my dad used to say, the grass is always greener on top of the septic tank."

> "Like my dad used to say, the grass is always greener on top of the septic tank."

This means that other opportunities frequently look better than staying where you are, but once you arrive at the new place and dig in, you'll discover the same problems or worse than what you've left.

You might be better off to double down on the investment you're making in the job you have.

Admittedly, when you're day-dreaming about a new job, you may overlook the value of staying with your organization, beyond that paycheck and insurance. Here are the top 10 reasons to stay:

1. **Leverage:** The longer you stay in a job, and the more wins you amass, the more trust and credits you have with which to negotiate on your own behalf. This leverage is helpful in requesting training, flexible work hours, modified work roles, assignment to exciting projects, and so on.
2. **Ease:** Red tape abounds in any organizational environment, but once you know a company, you know how to make things happen. At a new company you can expect to get bogged down for a while in alien systems and processes.
3. **Social Status:** You are more than your job title, but don't underestimate the perks of status, like the ease of introducing yourself at events or getting your LinkedIn invitations accepted.
4. **Trust:** When you work in an organization for a long time, you have the opportunity to build meaningful relationships. Being surrounded by a group of trusted colleagues is a wonderful experience and powerful motivation to stick around.
5. **Independence:** The first months in a new workplace are filled with learning the basics and asking questions at every

turn. It's a much better feeling to be the one who knows the job from A to Z.

6. **Confidence:** It's a confidence builder to be the expert, rather than the disoriented new person.

7. **Historical Knowledge:** "Knowing where the bodies are buried." When you have history in a workplace, you know which projects are black holes, and which offer real opportunities.

8. **Time-Off:** Years of service drives annual leave at many companies. At a new company, you'll have to start over.

9. **401(k) Vesting** – 401(k) matching often depends on years of service too. Matching may only begin after a set period, and some companies increase the matching the longer you stay. If you invest in them, they invest in you.

10. **Peace of Mind:** Changing jobs creates massive personal disruption and emotional costs, even if it increases your income.

You could leave your job and put your energy into creating the job you love somewhere else, but it might be smarter to capitalize on the opportunities where you are.

Sure, you may be thinking, I know there are all these benefits to staying where I am, but I still hate my job. I don't want to do this for another day, let alone the rest of my life.

We all have our fantasies about what we could only do if we left this place. But the reality is that often these fantasies simply lead to another manifestation of more of the same frustration—just at a different office.

So when you find yourself asking, "Should I stay or leave?" consider a more empowering alternative.

A More Empowering Alternative to the "Stay or Leave" Question

For a minute, shake yourself out of the internal debate of "should I stay or leave" because the narrowness of this perspective is a trap.

Staying implies that you've accepted the status quo and decided to put up with the same job frustrations. Leaving implies that the next job will turn out better.

But a superior solution usually lies between those perspectives, and it turns out that where you are is the best place for you to make a stand.

> When you decide to engage with the potential of your current job and cultivate the work that inspires you, good stuff happens.

Now, it won't necessarily happen like this for everyone, and it certainly won't happen overnight, but within six months, concrete results showed up for me:

- I received three awards from Executive Leadership for my leadership and results. Two of those awards came with financial rewards. (Note that in the previous five years with the same organization, I'd received zero recognition.)
- I was featured for the first time in our organization's newsletter, distributed to 100,000 employees, for results achieved on a major project.
- I received my biggest annual bonus ever and moved into a higher performing category in the organization, positioning me for promotion.
- My relationship and trust with the boss improved. We agreed to a more flexible work schedule and relocation to the city of my dreams.
- My staff meetings became much more fun and productive.

And my home life improved tremendously. I came home with renewed energy and excitement to share my "wins" for the day with my family—a routine we still have today. I began exercising again and living a healthier life.

The momentum carried me into new territory, as I began helping others through coaching, speaking, and blogging—activities that had never crossed my mind before.

I began to notice how many people showed up to work frustrated, "sleep working" through their days, scared about losing their jobs, and too scared to do anything about it.

I realized that I could help. These people are why I'm writing this book. But before you'll be able to put your heart into creating the job you love, you'll need to redefine two common beliefs about work that trip most people up (1) work is a grind, and (2) work is especially a grind at this company.

> you'll need to redefine two common beliefs about work that trip most people up (1) work is a grind, and (2) work is especially a grind at this company.

Chapter 3

REDEFINE YOUR BELIEFS ABOUT WORK

It ain't what you don't know that gets you into trouble.
It's what you know for sure that just ain't so.

Mark Twain

The first step on this journey is to take a serious look at your beliefs about work.

The two beliefs that stop most people are:

- Work is hard, tedious, never fun—an obligation to be met.
- You can't create a job to love in the company that currently employs you.

Redefining these two beliefs opens up opportunities to invest yourself, right where you are.

Our Two-Year Old Reveals the Ugly Truth

I woke up early and tired after a restless night of interrupted sleep, on autopilot, and getting ready for work. My two-year old ran to me and hugged my leg, crying, "Please don't leave."

Then the phrase slipped out of my mouth that I'd hoped never to hear. I haven't forgotten the moment:

Perhaps you've said that, too, but have you considered what this reveals about your beliefs? The beliefs that keep you trapped?

> "Honey, Daddy has to go to work."

The First Belief: Work is Inevitably "The Grind"

Business culture promotes the belief that work is a constant struggle and never fun. Consider our everyday language:

- "The Grind"
- "Another day, another dollar"

All those popular songs I loved, never noticing the beliefs they reinforced:

- "9 to 5" (What a way to make a living) - Dolly Parton
- "Take This Job and Shove It" - Johnny Paycheck and David Allen Coe
- "Daysleeper" - R.E.M.

Have you ever thought about the messages these songs reinforce while you're humming along?

Here are a couple of ways to redefine these titles:

- "9 to 5" (Is all about the living)
- "Take this Job, Then Create the One You Love"
- "Day-energetic"—still working on that one

But you get it. Society defines your beliefs about work unless you decide otherwise.

Your choice.

The Second Belief: You can't find a job to love at this company

Another common belief is that you can't create a job to love at the company where you work.

This belief is based on a very finite view of job positions and career progression. There are a couple of underlying ideas that support this belief that I'd like to debunk now by playing a quick game of True or False.

True or false:

> "My job description is what I actually do all day."
> *False. In my 16 years of work, I don't know a single person who actually does only the tasks in their job description.*

For proof, go ahead and pull out the job description from your hiring interview (most people can't even find it). Does this describe the job you do? In most cases, you'll probably recognize it doesn't. You've been performing a slightly or very different job the entire time.

The real job is probably a dynamic mix that reflects the needs of your boss, organization, and customers— and perhaps some of you mixed in there, too. They are a lot more fluid than we assume. Job descriptions are like "clay on the wheel" that we each mold to our own capabilities and the organization's needs.

> Job descriptions are like "clay on the wheel" that we each mold to our own capabilities and the organization's needs.

This means that you've got much more latitude than you realize to start incorporating work you love into your current job.

> "My job is to do just my work and nothing else."
> *False. In many companies, this kind of statement will get you a very low annual review rating and maybe even fired or forced into early retirement.*

Yes, the company needs you to do your job, but everybody knows that they expect more than that. I worked in a department where we all had five annual goals. The first goal was "Do Your Job." The other four were up for negotiation.

Because the expectation is for you to do more than your job, you have more opportunities to take on work you could love.

> "I'm only qualified to do a slightly more advanced version of what I did in the past."
> *False. There is a lot of confusion about "job experience." Most skills and experiences apply incredibly well to multiple areas of a company.*

If your background is Finance, consider whether IT people need help quantifying the impact of their projects and calculating the ROI of their software investments?

If you're in Marketing, do you think people in Finance and IT need help presenting their ideas?

If your background is HR, ask yourself whether project management needs help with its people? Wait—project management is mainly *about people.*

The point is that there are lots of ways to leverage your experience into different roles within the company, including plenty of hybrid possibilities.

The exciting part is to recognize that you can employ your skills and experiences in a variety of capacities. You can deliver a lot of value in a different capacity than you do now, all within the same company.

> "Even if I made a proposal to change my job to something I'm really excited about, no one would listen."
> *False. If you provide examples of how this change generates a return for your boss, your organization, and you, (in that order) most people will listen. Of course, that doesn't mean that the proposal immediately*

goes forward, but if the idea is compelling and helpful, you can usually get an audience.

This means that you can make changes to your job, especially if the value proposition is clear.

> You can make changes to your job, especially if the value proposition is clear.

So if your job description is just a starting point for your job, not the end point, what does that mean about the possibilities for creating something new for your work day?

Perhaps there isn't a job that you could love at your company today, but you can get busy creating it.

How to Redefine Your Work Beliefs

The good news is that you don't have to stay trapped in these messages.

Reconsider these beliefs and you open the door to reconnecting with your passion and, ultimately, to a job you will love.

Action Steps:

Step 1: Identify the Beliefs That Limit You

How you talk about your job reveals whether you've even given yourself permission to have a job you love. Consider "Dad gets to go to work" versus "Dad has to go to work."

> "Dad gets to go to work" versus "Dad has to go to work."

Hear the difference? One phrase says you're forced to go to work. The other frames your work as an opportunity.

Maybe that "have to go" language is a habit, but that's exactly the point. It's a habit that leads your mind, body, spirit, family, and coworkers to reinforce the negative messages.

Step 2: Expose Your Limiting Beliefs

Write down the name of one person you know who wildly loves his or her work. If you don't know anyone, visualize such a person. Write down the thoughts that come to mind. These notes may reveal your limiting beliefs about people who love their jobs.

Step 3: Question Your Limiting Beliefs

Why not you? Do you believe that having a job you love is just for the lucky or the privileged?

Question each limiting belief as it occurs to you. Enroll friends and family in supporting this exercise. Ask them to question it whenever you say, "I have to go to work." My wife and I still remind each other some mornings to say we "get" to go to work.

If self-reflection feels awkward, ask yourself whether you have the energy to question beliefs that diminish your potential for happiness and accomplishment.

Write down the name of the person from whom you learned your ideas about work. Your mom or dad or first boss? Consciously consider from whom you'd like to learn.

Step 4: Redefine Your Beliefs and Adopt a New Philosophy

Decide to see your job as a position from which to make an impact and learn about yourself. Decide that it is a place to stand, and worthy of investment.

Be patient. Adopting this new philosophy may take time. The rest of this book will help you develop the strategies and structure to support this step.

Give yourself permission to love your job. This act alone creates a small space for exploration and possibility, even if it sounds weird at first. When I started to question my beliefs, I was overwhelmed. I picked up a mantra from my friend Jonathan Mead (JonathanMead). com. He suggests that every time you find yourself thinking, "That's just the way it is," recite the mantra, "It's just a matter of time." It was very encouraging and kept me going.

> Give yourself permission to love your job.

> It's just a matter of time.

When You're Running From a Fire

It was my first call with my client, Andy. He had an MBA from Wharton and worked for one of the world's most prestigious consulting firms. It looked like he had everything going his way, but in our first call he said:

"Ben, I need to run from my job like I'm running from a fire."

He liked the financial benefits, but the work itself was draining every ounce of energy and happiness he had.

When we worked together, he began to uncover his belief that work was supposed to be this way, and he recognized that his belief prevented him from making changes in how he worked.

He began to question the beliefs that he couldn't take a lunch break, that he had to be on email until 11:30 p.m., and that disconnecting from work entirely on vacation was impossible.

The first exercise we did was a 10-minute lunch break in the park. He set the alarm on his phone and ate his sandwich without disturbance. He began to take lunch breaks away from his desk more frequently, which provided a refreshing break in his day. This led to his first vacation totally disconnected from work.

These steps gave him hope and restored his optimism that he could change his approach to work. This gave him momentum to make other changes at work. Amazing how just questioning and redefining a belief can make such an impact.

Once you begin to redefine these old beliefs—that work has to be a grind, and certainly at the company where you work—you'll find you can begin to shift your attitudes about who you are when you walk in that office door. You can begin to look more closely at your colleagues and the real needs of the company.

Chapter 4

TURN YOUR WORK INTO SOMETHING TO LOOK FORWARD TO

You don't need to be a genius or a visionary, or even a college graduate for that matter, to be successful. You just need framework and a dream.

Michael Dell

L ots of people view endless, repetitive meetings as a great example of "work as a grind."

I've studied how people show up to meetings, and there's good news.

Those meetings you've dreaded are actually a big opportunity for you to practice a career-saving, business-shifting, mind-blowing skill that will transform those meetings and the ways you habitually perceive the people and activities around you.

Doctor Jones, Doctor Jones

A few years ago I was exhausted from the litany of meetings and conference calls on my calendar. They were absolutely killing my work mojo. Then a friend suggested I show up differently.

The concept is to show up as someone who doesn't dread meetings. Think of someone whose way of being you'd like to express in place of dread.

I had nothing to lose, so I chose someone who embodies the spirit of adventure and excitement for me—Indiana Jones.

What was it like to be him in tough situations? How would he walk into the situation?

Indy never loses hope and always keeps his sense of humor and readiness to go for a new approach, especially when things look bleak.

Achieving New Results in the Same Old Meeting

I relished my first meeting as Indiana Jones. I asked questions differently, thought differently, even walked differently.

The results were far better and I had much more fun!

Clients to whom I've offered this approach have had positive results calling on:

- Rosie the Riveter, for toughness
- A father who stood up for what he believed in, for courage
- Nick Saban, for empowerment

What my friend didn't say was that when I showed up differently, I would perceive not only myself but everyone and everything around me differently. I would see opportunities where all I'd seen before were closed doors.

Action

Pick a meeting or another activity that you're dreading.

1. Consider which mood or essence you'd like to bring to the moment, i.e., empowerment, excitement, passion, curiosity, focus, or lightness.
2. Who embodies this?
3. Be that persona at your meeting.
4. Write down how it goes.

Taking on a new persona will open your eyes to possibility, I promise. The next step, one that will give you the tools to begin changing your work, involves lessons learned from a reality television show. But first, a case study.

> Taking on a new persona will open your eyes to possibility.

How to Have Your Best Work Year Ever

Elizabeth had worked for years as HR Director. She felt stuck, frustrated, and confined. Every night she went home sick from frustration.

We'd worked together and tried on a few personas for her work day, but nothing seemed the right fit.

Then we discovered the perfect persona, and that led to her best work year ever. She began listening differently. Instead of seeing the workplace in the context of HR challenges, she began to see new opportunities for building communication and trust across the organization's silos. Although she'd quit smoking years before, she walked out of staff meetings feeling like she wanted to "thump the butt" of a cigarette—euphoric!

> "thump the butt" of a cigarette—euphoric!

Her proposal to address the problems plaguing the organization resulted in a surprise $10,000 bonus and a recommendation to the board for her promotion to chief operating officer.

Let's talk about the television show persona that transformed Elizabeth.

Why I Always Cry During *Undercover Boss*

Every week on the reality television show, *Undercover Boss*, CEOs from companies like Chiquita, Subway, and Choice Hotels all go "undercover" to get their hands dirty working alongside their unsuspecting front line workers. The leaders gain full contact exposure to the real, everyday problems that their employees face.

The CEOs learn the basic rules of going undercover, apply them, and then discover new opportunities like:

- New product line ideas
- Working condition improvements for employees
- Process improvements to reduce costs

These discoveries often reignite the CEO's passion for the job, and they rediscover the joy of working.

The Three Essential Skills of the *Undercover Boss*

Elizabeth applied three skills learned from the *Undercover Boss* to identify the real problems that her coworkers and company face. Most people are more comfortable not noticing, but opportunities for promotion lie deeper. By adopting these new skills, she began to change who she was in the workplace, expanding her capacity to perceive what was actually occurring around her, and giving herself the opportunity to propose new steps to company leadership to address what she saw happening.

> Most people are more comfortable not noticing, but opportunities for promotion lie deeper.

Apply these skills like Elizabeth did, and you might find new opportunities that will reignite your passion for work and begin to set the course toward creating a job you will love.

#1 Immersion: It's essential to immerse yourself in your work day experience. A third-party consultant can never establish the trust and gain the insights you can through immersion. This means full commitment to the moment even during a week-long PowerPoint meeting or a two-hour conference call. The immersion state of mind means sitting up straight, leaning into the conversation, maintaining eye contact, taking notes, asking questions, and repeating back what you hear.

> The immersion state of mind means sitting up straight, leaning into the conversation, maintaining eye contact, taking notes, asking questions, and repeating back what you hear.

Action: Show Up Intentionally. Take a minute, before you walk through the door to your next meeting or dial the conference call number, and breathe deeply. Choose to show up curious and open to alternatives. If someone misses a deadline, ask why. If someone shows up angry or apathetic, ask why. Be willing to dig below the surface, and see what you can discover.

Action: Shut-up and Listen. Listen deeply to hear what's said. This can't happen if you're talking. In my undercover persona, I listen 80% of the time, ask questions 10%, and clarify the other 10%.

#2 Ignorance: Contrary to what you might assume, ignorance is an asset when undercover. In *Undercover Boss*, CEOs drop the tough façade and become students instead of teachers.

> In *Undercover Boss*, CEOs drop the tough façade and become students instead of teachers.

Action: Ask Questions and Hold the Space. When undercover, load your arsenal with powerful, open-ended questions, and then hold the space for answers. Don't have the answers? Be curious and liberal with questions. Even when you think you know the answer, ask a question to see what you might glean. Create the space, then wait and see what emerges.

Here are some sample questions:

- What are you bumping up against?
- What is the biggest challenge you and your team face?
- What would you most like to create next?
- If you wanted to go really big, what would you do?
- What risk would you like to take?

Action: Probe the Pain. When undercover, it's not enough to hear the problems and challenges. The next step is to probe the pain. When you hear about a problem, probe its significance, and ensure you understand its impact. Doing so helps you recognize your next best move.

Probe the pain by asking:

- What is the cost of this problem?
- What are its consequences?

Then take the questions deep and wide.

Deep questions probe and uncover more issues. For example, deep questions about turnover issues would be:

- What's the impact on productivity?
- What's the impact on training?
- What disruption does it cause?

Wide questions explore the impact of the challenge before and after an employee leaves:

- What happens before someone leaves?
- What happens afterwards?

#3 Adaptability and Endurance: The greatest challenge is learning to stick it out during extreme work situations like long periods of boredom and quickly changing environments. In *Undercover Boss*, CEOs are tested in both these situations, and many lose it. In the end, it's their reactions that break them, not the work or the problems. Endurance comes through practicing the art of staying undercover even when meetings run long or another fire drill erupts.

> Endurance comes through practicing the art of staying undercover even when meetings run long or another fire drill erupts.

Action: Build Your File of Opportunities. Once you apply these three skills—or go undercover, as I like to think of it—you're likely to find yourself overwhelmed by opportunities. File these for future reference. Many won't be worth taking on, but some you'll return to as golden.

I divided each page of a notebook down the middle with a line. On the left I wrote, "Problem," and on the right, "Pain." This tool served as a great reminder to listen for both the problem and the pain, no matter which conference call, conversation, or meeting I happen to be in.

Evernote increased my efficiency. I typed the problem/pain into a notes file on my phone and computer, and over time I built a file of opportunities easily searchable by keywords and by the source's name. I keep the Evernote app on my phone and computer so I can easily coordinate between them.

You can use any basic note-taking app that comes with most phones these days. The main point is that when undercover, it's empowering to pull out my phone and type in the problem and pain for future reference. Avoid napkins, business cards, and backs of envelopes—they are too easy to misplace.

How I Discovered My Biggest Opportunity During the Meeting from Hell

I had third-row floor seats with my wife to the Avett Brothers, perhaps my favorite band. Then the boss called, and my heart sank.

"Ben, we need you to fly out for a meeting."

Arrrrrgh!

I hated to miss the great evening we had planned for months in exchange to travel to another city and sit through a week's worth of depressing PowerPoints in the dark. I was exchanging Heaven for Hell.

In my disappointment, all I could think was, "This better be worth it."

I complained to my coach about this trip and how once again my boss had overruled my personal life.

My coach didn't commiserate but suggested that instead of whining, I accept the situation and adopt the role of going undercover.

I filled a notebook with challenges that my coworkers were facing. I took it as an opportunity to probe the pain of the problem.

I kept hearing that our team wasn't getting results or meeting deadlines. Normally, I would have viewed this as just another complaint from leadership about productivity. However, when I looked deeper, I saw the project pipeline was full, but delivery wasn't timely. The issue looked like a misunderstanding about "project completion."

I volunteered to lead a series of six lunch-and-learns about getting results. One of the main elements was having conversations with your boss to clarify and negotiate goals. The outcome of these lunches was that our team improved its communication and performance.

Plus, this was work that inspired me!

Going undercover doesn't always have the intended outcome—at least not right away. Complaints about long working hours had reached fever pitch in one of my work groups. I decided to survey 20 of my coworkers, informally and anonymously. I found that:

- 80% were staying late more than three days per week
- 80% were taking conference calls before 8:00 a.m. and after 6:00 p.m.
- Only 10% found their work environment inspiring
- 80% didn't believe or weren't sure if they had a future with the company
- 70% would consider leaving if offered the same position and pay at another company

I wasn't surprised, considering national trends. I created a proposal to address burnout and turnover for my company and quantified the impact at more than $3.6 million.

The discussion around this proposal is still on-going, but I build that file every day. It's just a matter of time!

(For an example of an informal survey you can create with a simple Excel spreadsheet and a proposed template, visit BenFanning.com/quit.)

Now, imagine how invigorating your work day could be if you were working on something like this that inspires you and promises to benefit your organization too.

How I Became a Burnout Specialist

Eventually, I leveraged what I learned when I went undercover during the "meeting from hell" to make a meaningful impact within the organization. I understood the cost of turnover and disengagement, and I knew I could help. This eventually led to my making an offer to my organization to coach other employees one-on-one, lead lunch-and-learns, and work with larger groups.

You can see that trying on a different persona at work can be a lot of fun, and that adopting the three undercover boss techniques may lead you to discover a boatload of opportunity.

Then, once you act on the opportunities for which you have passion—presto, you transition to becoming an employee with more mojo and motivation.

In the next chapter let's dive deeper into motivation, which happens to be the place to start to create the job you love.

SECTION II

Cultivate the Work
That Inspires You

In this section, you'll discover your inner motivation for working, identify the kind of work that offers you a dose of motivation, and then kick off your campaign for more of the work you love.

Let's go!

Chapter 5

UNLOCK YOUR SECRET SOURCE OF MOTIVATION

Motivation is a fire from within. If someone else tries to light that fire under you, chances are it will burn very briefly.

Stephen R. Covey, The 7 Habits of Highly Effective People

S he was my first direct report, and every day was a battle between us. She'd worked at the company for years, and I was a young, paranoid manager.

It all came to a head over one of the most grueling certifications imaginable—Customs Compliance.

I wouldn't see her with that certification unless I had mine, too. It was the most brutal exam for which I'd ever prepared, and it took every ounce of energy I had. I spent weekends miserably preparing, fueled only by anger, frustration, and the sheer will to compete.

I missed passing by two points. My direct report didn't pass either, but immediately began studying for the next exam. I closed my books and never opened them again.

She was internally motivated and eventually passed. I was externally motivated—by competition and fear—and when I failed, quickly lost my mojo.

Tap Into a Deeper Source of Motivation

A couple of years later I finally understood. I had a newborn baby, a full-time job, a budding coaching practice on the side, and a new blog.

This scenario could have become another customs exam but didn't because this time I was motivated from within—to provide for my new family and to solve a problem that I was passionate about, a problem whose impact I'd experienced personally and seen my coworkers struggle with—burnout.

I was burning the candle at both ends, sleeping less than I had in years, but I sustained my motivation to keep going.

> It makes a big difference when your motivation comes from within.

Unmotivated Monday Mornings

We dread Mondays when we don't feel motivated. Monday Mornings give lots of people the blues.

- The *American Journal of Hypertension* reported that many workers suffer a significant increase in blood pressure returning to the office after the weekend.
- The phrase, "having a case of the Mondays," is shorthand for grumpiness.
- And consider the many songs inspired by melancholy Mondays, like "Manic Monday" by the Bangles, and "Monday, Monday" by the Mamas and Papas.

One study found that on average a professional cracks his or her first smile on Monday morning at 11:16 a.m., according to the UK publication, *The Telegraph*.

Maybe you head to work on Monday to appease the boss, lay the groundwork for a raise, or slog through that project hanging over your head.

Yes, those are motivating factors, but they are not sustainable. It's like losing weight for a class reunion or a beach trip.

Daniel Pink, in his book *Drive*, says that most people think about motivation as something done to them or done for others. So instead, let's consider motivation as *internally sourced*.

What if your motivation for weight loss was internally sourced? From a deeper place? Lose weight to be there for your family or as your children grow up, get married, and have children themselves. Or being a role model of health and wellness for those around you?

> What if your motivation for weight loss was internally sourced?

See the difference?

Simon Sinek, author of *Start with Why and Leaders Eat Last*, defines "why" as "to live with a sense of purpose, cause, or belief." The simplest way to define your internal motivation for going to work is to find the reason why you work in the first place: your internal and deeper motivation for the long haul.

Does your motivation to go to work on Monday begin to shift slightly if you think about setting an example for your children, helping the coworkers you've worked alongside for years, or because your job is preparing you for the next step in your career?

> Find the reason why you work in the first place: your internal and deeper motivation for the long haul.

Go even deeper. How about if you're working to achieve what you once thought was impossible, to do more of the work you love, or maybe you're the kind of person who finishes what you start?

ACTION: Identify Your Source of Internal Motivation

Write down a time in your life when you had a big project or other extra responsibilities. Was it difficult or easy to get motivated? Was your motivation internal or external? What internal motivations would have inspired you?

ACTION: Seeing the Forest for the Trees Exercise

Write on a Post-it® note why you show up at the office every morning. Stick the Post-it® on your bathroom mirror, car dashboard, or suitcase as a reminder to connect with the bigger picture. Understand why you work, and you can use these inspirational ideas to motivate yourself when the going gets tough, like Jim did.

A Reminder During the Heat of the Battle

Jim was five years from retirement but wasn't sure he could hang on. He experienced every day as an emotional roller coaster. One minute he felt on top of things, making an impact. The next minute he was rearranging chairs on the *Titanic*.

If he couldn't hang in there until retirement, he questioned whether he should look for a job elsewhere, even at lower pay.

That's when we created together a simple reminder of why he was working. He listed three reasons why on a Post-it® note on his computer monitor:

- Financial security
- His team and coworkers
- The bigger impact he hoped to make in the world

Even during the worst fire drills at the office, his reasons why pulled him back to focus on the task at hand.

Baby Steps to Build Momentum

Tapping those deep sources of motivation, like so many big changes, often begins with baby steps.

Choose one of these strategies:

> Take a baby step by beginning each morning in a way that will create momentum to carry you through the day.

1. Organize the day to make things happen

I picked up this motivational tip from Seth Godin, author of *Linchpin*. Instead of approaching each morning reviewing what you have to do, start with what you want to make happen. Consider which of these approaches yields the most energy and inspiration for your Monday morning:

> #1: Check-off the to-do list: respond to emails, anticipate obstacles, pay bills, and complete your annual goals.

> or

> #2: Set big goals, take risks, give more than you take, organize a community, create a new possibility, and demand excellence.

Which one would inspire you?

2. Redesign your defaults

What's your office routine? Ever sit in front of the computer all day because that's what you're accustomed to doing?

Do you check email every five minutes? (That's 24,000 times per year, feeling a pulse of dread every time the "ding" of a new email arrives.)

Change your defaults. Rise from your desk every few hours, unplug, and take a walk. Or stop eating at your desk and go to the breakroom, if not outdoors.

3. Start your to-do list with "why"

When you turn to the to-do list in the morning with a sense of dread, it's time for a change. Writing this book, I lost track of why I was writing it, and I began to dread the writing. What helped was taking out my to-do list and writing out the importance of each item. Doing this helped me prioritize and even eliminate items. It helped me push through places I was stuck.

4. Connect with one inspiring person

To motivate yourself and put a spring in your step as you arrive at the office, don't look at the to-do list.

Start your day connecting with one inspiring person. No matter what your environment is like, you can identify energizing and inspiring people.

> Start your day connecting with one inspiring person.

Plan and schedule your first interactions of the day. Not much is worse than starting your day at the office with a discouraging conference call or a negative hallway interaction.

Set up a coffee or a conference call with someone upbeat and creative. This step is a low-stress self-motivator because all it requires is planning and showing up.

Connecting with your family at home is a great way to get motivated, too. Our family often breakfasts together, holding our own breakfast party. It starts our day positively and the momentum we gain carries over into work and school.

If you're struggling to think this through, here are a couple of steps I learned from Scott Dinsmore at LiveYourLegend.net in his article,

"Your 1st Step: Find One Person Who Inspires Possibility." He took this simple process and orchestrated an amazing global meet-up across 44 countries and 2,000 people all on the same day. Talk about motivation!

> "Who do you look up to? Who do you admire, or maybe even envy (in a healthy, excited way)? We all have at least one person—a friend, colleague, family member. Or maybe a friend of a friend through someone else in your life.
>
> Pick one of those people and make a conscious effort this week to hang out with him or her—invite them to a lunch or a workout or just give them a call. Maybe even tell them your plan to transform your surroundings and that they're high on the list. That can be the ultimate compliment.
>
> Can't think of someone? First try harder. If that doesn't work, then go to where the inspiring people hang out. Find an event in town, join a group on Meetup.com or check out Craigslist. Every town, big or small, has a ton of options.
>
> *Reserve an hour this week to find that one person and spend a little time with them. See what happens."*

5. Know exactly what you'll work on before sitting down

Not much is less motivating than sitting at your desk not knowing exactly what you're about to work on. Avoid these minutes of hesitation with one of these techniques:

a. The Ernest Hemingway Technique:

Nothing motivates you on Monday morning like momentum, as the famous writer Ernest Hemingway understood.

He left the last chapter or paragraph unfinished at the end of each day, especially when he knew exactly how it would end. So when he sat down at his desk the next day, he could immediately start writing. He never sat at his desk wondering what to write next.

Instead of staying late on Friday or working over the weekend to wrap up a task, pick a strategic place to stop, so when you arrive on Monday, you know exactly what's next. This momentum will carry you through the day.

b. Five First Steps

When you know exactly what your first task will be, you're more motivated to get to the office. Write out the first five to ten steps of the day in detail, either right before leaving the office or on first waking up the next morning.

I stick a Post-it® note listing my first steps of the day on my laptop, and then execute them once I arrive at my desk. This strategy fires your mind quickly into execution mode and boosts confidence for tackling any big issues that arise later in the day.

c. Review Your To-Do List First

This is a tip I picked up from one of the most prolific bloggers and content creators, Chris Brogan, who advises large Internet organizations like Google with several books, including a best seller. Before you check email or social media, always glance *first* at your to-do list. This simple default keeps you focused on your first priorities, whether business or personal, and protects you from the time-sucking minutia of work and social media.

You've just learned the importance of finding what motivates you, and some guidance for taking the first baby steps toward creating momentum. The next chapter explores how to discover deeper sources of motivation in your work life and identify the kinds of work that motivate you.

Chapter 6

DISCOVER THE WORK THAT MOTIVATES YOU

The biggest mistake people make is not making a living at doing what they most enjoy.

Malcolm Forbes, Publisher of Forbes Magazine

N ow that you've taken a few baby steps toward motivation, it's time to call on that new energy to get serious about finding what will motivate you more deeply in your workplace—what is the work that energizes you and how can you secure more of it—as you begin to create the job you love.

Work doesn't feel like work when you discover the deeper sources of motivation in your work place.

How the Threat of Outsourcing Helped Me Stumble into Work That Fired Up My Motivation

Fresh out of college, I was an industrial engineer. I went full force into becoming the best industrial engineer I could.

I did time studies, evaluated manufacturing plant layouts, and invested hours of energy into spreadsheets. My hands ached from typing.

For some people, this would be a dream job, but heavy analysis and quiet computer time left my energy on empty. I had to invest twice the effort of other engineers—who loved it—and I went home depleted and exhausted.

A few years later, I discovered by chance what I loved to do, rediscovering my motivation, and as a result energizing my day like never before.

My boss assigned me to lead a project on the brink of failure. Two coworkers had failed. The project was to outsource part of our analytical work to a team in India. My mission was to train that team, check their work, and determine how fast the transition could go.

I dreaded the additional work load and the 7:00 a.m. conference calls. Plus the writing was on the wall that we'd all be outsourced, so why bother?

Half-heartedly, I began to train them at 7:00 a.m. each morning—and I loved it.

Although I didn't enjoy the tasks I was training them to perform, the act of training people invigorated me. I enjoyed preparing the training documents, delivering the content, and charting their progress.

I didn't mind waking up early and putting in the extra time. I always felt motivated and energized for my day afterwards. (The project succeeded, by the way.)

The Pandora's Box I'd opened was that finally I knew the work that motivated me and energized me far more effectively than coffee or Red Bull ever could.

> When your day is full of motivating work, it doesn't feel like work.

3 Easy Steps to Finding the Work That Motivates You

When your day consists of work that you are motivated to do, it doesn't feel like work.

What I had to determine next was how to do more of the work that inspired and energized me and less of the work that exhausted me.

Step 1: List all your work activities.

Write down everything you do at work for at least eight hours—a few days is best. Keep the list on your desk, in your pocket, or planner. Note the types of emails, phone calls, conversations, projects, meals, issues—everything you do, in detail.

You'll quickly observe that everything listed either inspires or drains you.

Step 2: Classify each activity as inspiring or required and exhausting.

Review the list and classify each activity with a "+" for inspiring or a "–" for required and exhausting.

'+' is an activity that inspires you. You invest effort and focus, but the energy return is immediate. In the middle of the activity, you may enter a "flow state" where you are so immersed that you lose track of space and time. When done, you feel lighter and more alive. Just by examining my day, I quickly saw what inspired and filled my soul: starting the morning with an upbeat meeting over coffee, teaching, presenting on a new topic, and leading a meeting.

'–' is an activity required by your job that exhausts you. I quickly identified these soul-sucking activities, too. You're required to invest your energy but without the energy payback. You may feel like you need coffee or a nap afterwards to recoup. For me, those daily tasks were: the morning commute, Excel reporting, answering emails, sitting through a routine meeting, eating lunch at my desk, and building an Access database.

Your list will differ from mine. What matters is that after this exercise, you'll have a list unique to you of activities that fill your soul and those that drain you.

Here are a couple of tips:

1. **Notice:** No activity is neutral. Everything either inspires and energizes you or drains and weighs you down with obligation. Notice.
2. **Don't blame the work:** The work is innocent. The designations of inspired or exhausting reflect your response, not the work itself. Work that inspires you, drains someone else. The work that drains you energizes someone out there—find that person!
3. **Disregard the guilt:** For me, the hardest part was permitting myself to be honest about what motivated and what exhausted me. I felt guilty that so many of an engineer's traditional duties exhausted me. Honesty allowed me to articulate my preferences to my boss and begin to shift my role towards energizing work.

The immediate challenge I faced was that more of my activities featured minus signs than pluses. I quickly understood why I was coming home with so little energy to exercise, cook dinner, or be genuinely present with my family.

I saw that there was one more step to take to create the job I love.

Step 3: Master the Inspired Work Ratio

The inspired work ratio is the balance between work that inspires and work that doesn't.

So…

Inspired work hours: Required work hours

Add up the pluses and minuses on your list.

Required Work Hours > Inspiring Work Hours = Exhausted by 5:00 p.m.

Inspiring Work Hours > Required Hours = Energized by 5:00 p.m.

If inspired hours exceed required hours at the end of the day, you will feel better and carry momentum out the door.

Review the list to see which activities you could tweak, negotiate, or restructure:

> Examine your ratio between the activities that inspire and those that exhaust you, so you can plan your next move.

- **Look for the small, energizing modification.** Sometimes you can flip an activity from required to energizing simply by modifying it. For example, using Excel or PowerPoint all day completely exhausts me, but using them to illustrate a teaching point engages me. Even when the day is full of required activities, and I finish exhausted, I feel better knowing why. I understand what happened and make modifications for tomorrow.
- **Collaborate for more motivating work.** Your list differs from your coworker's. Create a win-win by offering to do work that motivates you in exchange for a coworker doing your required work. I did this when I trained the India team, and my coworkers handled analytical requests that came in. My coworkers were happier, and I was excited to do more of the work that made me come alive.
- **Notice how people impact your energy.** You can't always choose your coworkers, but when you can, intentionally decide to spend time with people who boost your energy rather than bring you down.
- **Restructure your work day to build momentum.** For many people, it may not be realistic to fill the day with

inspired work. Sometimes investing in soul-sucking activities will earn you those inspired hours. Structure your work day to include enough motivation to carry you through. Here are a few scheduling ideas:

Ideal times to schedule work that motivates you:

- The moment you walk into the office
- The first task after lunch
- Immediately after the most tedious work you do
- Immediately before leaving the office for the day

Ideal times to schedule your required work:

- The first task waking up with the first cup of coffee (yes, caffeine's involved)
- The second task of the day after you're off to a good start Saturday or Sunday morning, with a day of energizing activity ahead that you're eagerly anticipating
- Immediately before the deadline. A required stop time focuses you and prevents the work from dragging on. I personally find this strategy very useful

How to Increase Your Motivation for Walking In the Office Door

When I started working with Jen, she faced an internal energy crisis, reporting in our first conversation that she was registering only 3 out of 10 in terms of her own motivation at work. Her productivity was down, and she even found herself intentionally taking the long way to work every morning to give herself extra time to muster the energy to walk through the office door.

We reviewed her daily activities and discovered that her lack of motivation was mostly the result of changes in those activities. Due to shifts across the organization, she had taken on more of the required work that drained her. She did it because it had to get done, and she knew she could do it, but it drained her.

We put a plan in place to manage her required work load and increase the work that inspired her. Within a few weeks, she reported that her energy was consistently registering 7 out of 10—more than double!

Her renewed motivation and energy boosted her productivity and helped her enjoy her work day much more. Her relationships at work improved, since she now had the motivation and energy to invest.

Time to Get More of the Work that Inspires

Now it's time to take what you've learned about the work that inspires you and the work that drains you, and go out deliberately to secure more work that inspires you and keep shifting that ratio in a positive direction.

Chapter 7

CAMPAIGN FOR THE WORK YOU LOVE

Before dreaming about the future or making plans, you need to articulate what you already have going for you—as entrepreneurs do.

Reid Hoffman, LinkedIn co-founder

Motivating work plays to your natural strengths, passion, and skills; it's the energizing and soul-filling work that you discovered in Chapter 6. Spending the day on motivating work requires less effort, and you'll find yourself more confident and more inclined to be generous with your time.

The reality, though, is that getting more work that motivates you won't happen by luck. Campaigning for it will help you create the job you love.

The result is a happier work day and continual progress towards a more satisfying career.

> Campaigning means owning your power to make this happen. It's imposing your will on the job, instead of allowing the job to impose its will on you.
>
> Campaigning is even a line of defense against an overload of work assignments that may be mandatory but also drain the life out of you.

Unfortunately, many employees never discover their power to accomplish this shift. They remain trapped in the perspective that they must do whatever the boss hands down to them or what the job description spells out. Yes, of course, the boss's requests and the company's expectations matter, but you aren't captive to these.

In particular, please don't advertise that you're happy doing work you hate.

Stop Advertising That You're Happy Doing Work You Hate

My client, Sam, couldn't understand why he kept getting the same kind of tedious assignments over and over. It wasn't that he hated his job or the company, he was just sick of these assignments.

You see, he always got the job done and put on a happy face every Monday when he reported his results in the staff meeting.

His boss and coworkers had no idea he was so frustrated, because he masked it so well. He was under the impression that if he endured this grinding work long enough, he'd finally get to do the kind of work he loved. Instead, everyone was happy to let him continue completing those assignments because he was good at it and because his coworkers didn't want to do that kind of work either.

> He'd unknowingly been campaigning that he was happy doing work he hated.

The solution wasn't for Sam to start whining about this work, doing it poorly, or stop doing it altogether. All he needed to do was just stop talking about it.

So instead of talking up his wins at the staff meeting in those assignments he hated, he gave updates on work he actually liked doing. Sometimes it seemed he was highlighting the smallest of

76

achievements, but eventually he began to see more assignments he liked coming his way and fewer of the ones he didn't.

I was a lot like Sam. Looking back, I did a lot of grunt work that no one else wanted but the fundamental problem was that I acted like I loved that grunt work, and I was so convincing that it just kept coming.

Ironically, thanks to my promoting this work on my annual review, resume, and LinkedIn profile, I ended up managing an entire team of people doing the work, which escalated my frustration—and theirs.

And I honestly couldn't stop because my professional identify and financial rewards were all wrapped up in this work. This led to sleepless nights, dreaded Monday mornings, and plenty of unhappy hours.

To create the job you love, stop advertising your exceptional results for the required work that wears you out, and start campaigning for more of the work that inspires and motivates you.

7 Steps to Campaign For the Work That Inspires You

Begin your campaign with a few steps:

1. Clarify which tasks deplete you. Everyone finds some aspects of their job to be a grind, but most people don't take the time to figure out exactly which tasks these are. Become aware of which activities drain and deplete you.

Action: List the top three tasks that deplete your motivation and are required aspects of your job. (Refer to Chapter 6.)

2. Clarify which tasks motivate you. Sometimes it's more difficult to recognize which work motivates you because what plays to your strengths and passions may become invisible to you.

A client once sent me his three-page resume in advance of our working together. When I asked him about all the achievements he'd listed, he explained that although he was proud of it all, he hadn't enjoyed most of what he'd done. I asked him to go back through the resume and take out everything he didn't enjoy and send it back to me. He whittled the three pages down to one-quarter of a page.

We worked together to build an entirely new resume expanding on that one-quarter page. He ended up with a resume that highlighted the work that motivated him.

He said, "Ben, reading my resume used to depress me. Now I'm motivated by reading it. I keep it by my bed to read when I wake up in the morning to motivate me for my work day."

Could you imagine reading your resume when you wake up to motivate yourself to go to work?

Action: List the top three work tasks that motivate you.

3. Plant the seed with your boss.
Start a conversation by talking about the work that motivates you. Many employees just assume the boss knows what they're good at and enjoy—a risky assumption. Unless you articulate what motivates you, most bosses will assign whatever seems like a good fit or whatever they'd prefer not to do themselves. Give your boss examples of work that you would like more of.

> Many employees just assume the boss knows what they're good at and enjoy—a risky assumption.

Action: List three tasks that you'd like to be assigned more often. Write them down as concise bullet points to have as a reference for your next conversation with the boss. Sometimes it's helpful to plant the seed with your boss by first introducing this idea in a casual conversation over lunch or coffee. This approach yields initial feedback that will help you plan your strategy for a more formal conversation. Wrap up your casual conversation by noting that you'll schedule time to discuss in more depth later. Note that although you may be tempted to wait until your annual performance review, I recommend talking sooner so that your new goals will reflect any changes.

By mentioning this idea casually at first, you may inspire your boss to think it was her idea to give you more work that you love!

4. Establish your track record. Volunteer to help someone complete work that they are required to do but comes easily (and happily) to you. People with different skills are everywhere throughout your organization, and you can increase your list of wins in acquiring the work that you want more of by offering to help. For example, if you see coworkers struggling with a presentation or an analysis, offer to help if it's in the

> you can increase your list of wins in acquiring the work that you want more of by offering to help.

sweet spot of the work you'd like more of. Ask them to let the group or the boss know that you helped, which will both build goodwill and your reputation for a type of work that you love.

This step is incredibly helpful. When I was interested in coaching inside my company, I first offered to mentor a few new hires. This offer built my track record of success in helping others, which led to mentoring becoming part of my formal job responsibilities within the year.

Action: Write down the last time you enjoyed helping someone. Now go back to that person and offer to help again.

5. Highlight your motivating achievements, and minimize the required ones. Most people highlight all their accomplishments in their annual review, resume, and LinkedIn profile. This is a major mistake. The consequence is that the work that really motivates you never stands out. Make sure that the work you love gets the most real estate.

> Make sure that the work you love gets the most real estate.

My friend in accounting bragged that he was in the top 10 percent of all viewed LinkedIn profiles. I knew he didn't like his work and wanted to do something different within his company, so I asked him who was viewing his profile. Accounting Recruiters. He'd unknowingly been campaigning for more accounting jobs and attracting people who wanted to hire accountants. With a few modifications, we started his campaign for a new and more motivating line of work within his current company.

Action: Pull up your most recent resume or LinkedIn profile. Notice how much space you allocate to work that you love versus work that leads to frustration. Make sure to emphasize, allocate the most space, and place at the top of the page the work that you love.

6. Modify the work you're required to do to make it motivating. It may not be realistic to eliminate all the work that wears you out, but modify it to play to your strengths. The only way I could survive an Excel analysis was to schedule a presentation to share

> It may not be realistic to eliminate all the work that wears you out, but modify it to play to your strengths.

the findings. I could then approach the Excel task with more enthusiasm. On the other hand, I've had clients who enjoyed preparing presentations but dreaded presenting. They invested their time up front and actually recorded part of their presentation in advance so they could play it back to the audience, and then offer a live Q&A. I've also had clients break down their presentations into group exercises so they would be speaking formally only briefly. All these actions modify the work you have to do and make it more motivating.

Action: Consider how you could slightly modify each task listed in Step 1 to play more to your strengths.

7. Collaborate with coworkers who like to do the tasks you're required to perform. Avoid complaining, but attentively stay on the lookout for collaborators with different skills who would love the tasks that deplete you. Tap the strengths of your coworkers. Ask them which tasks are the easiest for them as well as the most difficult, and then explore how you could collaborate to help one another.

> Tap the strengths of your coworkers.

This step might sound unusual, and that's because it is. There's a mentality out there that we should all strive to be good at everything instead of tapping into each other's strengths.

I saw a perfect example of this just the other day. One of my clients has to run a third-party software to coordinate bidding activity. He loves to work with the vendors but abhors dealing with the clunky software. He found someone else on the team who prefers staying in his office operating software rather than being out front with the vendors. My client is helping him deal with the vendors, and he now runs the software on all bidding. By collaborating, both are doing less of the work they dislike and more of what they enjoy.

Action: List your three closest coworkers. What are they naturally good at, and what are their biggest challenges? Where could you help them most? Where could they help you?

Now it's time for the next step to sustain your momentum toward more motivating work.

Ten Strategies to Boost Your Reputation and Become an Expert

Another effective way to campaign for motivating work is by boosting your reputation and becoming an expert. Becoming an expert at work that inspires you provides job security and leverage to negotiate on your own behalf to create the job you love.

> Becoming an expert at work that inspires you provides job security and leverage to negotiate on your own behalf to create the job you love.

Here are ten strategies for becoming an expert at work that inspires and motivates you. Some of these strategies might seem over the top for someone working within an organization, but the good news is that you don't have to do them all to establish yourself as an expert. Taking on one or two will set you apart.

1. Do the motivating work exceptionally well. When you perform very well, you become known as the person to turn to for similar assignments in the future.

2. Talk up your motivated work wins. Share your excitement over wins doing work you love in meetings, conference calls, lunches, and happy hours.

3. Write and present on your motivating work wins. Volunteer to write a case study for your company's website or newsletter.

4. Quantify, quantify, quantify. Numbers often speak louder than words inside an organization. Measure and calculate the impact of the work. These become great points to emphasize in your annual review, resume, and LinkedIn profile. Even if you're not a huge Excel fan (like me), it's time to dust off your skills

> You can quantify and call out impact in any of these areas to make a powerful statement:

and get to quantifying. You can quantify and call out impact in any of these areas to make a powerful statement:

- Revenue: How does your motivating work increase revenue for the company?
- Cost savings: How does your motivating work save the company money versus what was spent in the past?
- Cost avoidance: How does it avoid cost increases that you anticipate in the future?
- Pay terms: How will it help your company get paid more easily or more quickly?
- Customer satisfaction: How does it help retain customers or encourage them to buy more?
- Employee retention: How does it reduce employee turnover or increase their engagement? How does it increase their productivity?
- Idea generation: How does it increase creativity, ideas for new products, or potential solutions?
- Cycle time: How does it affect the speed to market of new products or processing of new orders?
- Quality: How does it get better products out more consistently?

5. Share how it helps your boss, department, and coworkers. In addition to quantifying the impact, it's important to underscore the benefits to the people you work alongside. When they benefit from you doing motivating work, they'll be more likely to support you going forward.

- Visibility: Does it promote other accomplishments of the group?
- Ease: Does it ease the work day for those around you?
- Bigger and Better: Will it lead to even bigger results for the team?

6. Speak at town hall meetings. Offer to share a case study (code for the story of a win in your motivating work area) at a town hall meeting in front of the organization.

7. Contribute to company forums. Share helpful news and tips about your specialty area on the company's forums, including the intra-web and company LinkedIn group. (Consider starting one if the company doesn't have one.) The beautiful part is that you can just share industry news or articles in the area you want to move into, and this will boost your expert status.

8. Build your network in an area outside the organization. Look up LinkedIn groups in your interest area and mix it up online. Seek out related conferences so you can build relationships with experts outside of your company.

9. Get interviewed in the media. Sometimes you have to run this by your company first, but doing interviews in your area of expertise builds your reputation internally, too.

10. Speak at conferences. Public speaking in general boosts your reputation as an expert, but speaking on a larger platform helps it grow more quickly—especially when you speak with other experts at a conference or on a panel.

> Public speaking in general boosts your reputation as an expert.

For instance, Annie's most motivating work occurred when she worked directly with external vendors and customers to solve problems. The challenge was that most of her job was sitting behind her desk on the computer. She was an introvert and had a reputation as someone content to stay in her office all day, but this just wasn't the case. Her campaign for getting more of the work she loved started when she volunteered to speak on an industry panel at a conference. Then she forwarded the conference link around her organization. Her colleagues began to perceive her as an expert, and she started to receive invitations to participate in more external meetings, which she loved. She began to find her work day far more motivating.

Note that although I list strategies to build your reputation both inside and outside the company, organizations often place greater value on building your expert status outside the company. The takeaway is to work through both channels.

Now to Getting More of the Work You Love

Now that you've started your campaign for more motivating work, we'll talk in the next chapter about how all this "taking care of yourself" does not have to cost your company or your coworkers. In fact, you may discover that the pursuit of the win-win-win (your boss-your company-you) will mean even more work that you love.

SECTION III

Create and Sustain the Job You Love

Now that you're making progress towards creating the job you love, we'll start to apply the skills to help you sustain your gains and make your job even better.

As I mentioned in the Foreword, the skills required for creating a job are very different than those for finding one. Finding a job involves networking, interviewing, and selling yourself, but the strategies I share here are frequently underutilized or not utilized at all, yet are essential for creating and sustaining the job you love.

I'll share with you how to negotiate without your boss or company losing, own the effectiveness of your messages, bring your personal side to work, and finally, revitalize a dead office into an inspiring place to work.

Ready, set, go!

Chapter 8

NEGOTIATE—
WITHOUT OTHERS LOSING

*You can have everything in life you want, if you will just help others
get what they want.*

Zig Ziglar

An essential skill for sustaining the job you love is learning to go after what you want without costing your boss or your company what they want.

Negotiating a win for yourself does not mean that someone else has to lose. You can learn to find or create an equal exchange of value that's satisfactory for the boss, the organization, and yourself—also known as the win-win-win.

> You can learn to find or create an equal exchange of value that's satisfactory for the boss, the organization, and yourself—also known as the win-win-win.

This approach generates more trust, better relationships, and more likelihood of sustaining the job you love.

Although today negotiation is part of my daily routine, it took an awkward experience on the company jet for me to realize its potential value.

The Day I Learned That Everything is Negotiable

I was a road-weary business traveler about to make my third trip in a month to Latin America. Just as I was booking my flight, I received an email that the corporate jet happened to be headed for the same destination.

I immediately arranged my first flight on the corporate jet. I was so excited I could barely contain myself. The day of my flight, I arrived so early that I beat the pilots and everyone else to the airport. When the pilot opened the plane, I landed in a plush leather seat right up front.

One-by-one, top executives boarded. I'd seen their photos on our website, but never met them in person. It was a moment of triumph, and I personally greeted each one. We were set to go with a full flight, when another executive arrived as the doors were closing. No seats left, or so I thought.

The good news was that I didn't get kicked off the flight. The late-boarding executive directed me to the bathroom, where I sat on the toilet for the two-hour flight, except when it was in use, and I stood waiting in the aisle.

> The late-boarding executive directed me to the bathroom, where I sat on the toilet for the two-hour flight, except when it was in use, and I stood waiting in the aisle.

I could have experienced this as profoundly humiliating. I could have stormed out and flown commercial as usual. But that day I came to understand a fundamental principle. I'd operated under the impression that corporate was a rigid place to work, but I discovered I could get what I wanted so long as I helped others get what they wanted, too. Turns out that everything is negotiable.

> Turns out that everything is negotiable.

The executive team met together in comfort. I got what I wanted—exchanging a ten-hour flight ordeal for an easy two-hour trip with many of our company's executives.

Plus, I left with a memorable story that I called upon to break the ice in a future conversation to ask the company to help pay for my MBA. More about that shortly.

Once you recognize that everything is negotiable, the next step is to adopt a negotiation perspective every day.

See what happened for my client, Susan.

Adopting a Negotiation Perspective Without Disrespecting Anyone

Susan was sitting at her computer when an email came across from her boss.

"Susan, we need to take a look at your job. They may need you back in Accounting."

She called me in a panic. "I knew it. They want me to go back to doing accounting work! Just more robotic button pushing."

She'd spent years making her way out of Accounting and creating the job she loved doing corporate sales and hospitality. She'd heard the rumblings that they needed help in Accounting urgently, and she was afraid. Now that she'd created the job she loved, she didn't want to lose it.

She immediately went to LinkedIn and started looking at the job boards. She knew if she let this happen, she would be resentful and increasingly angry.

But after our conversation, she decided to wait before applying for other jobs and to ask Accounting, "How can I help?"

She discovered that the Accounting department had suffered a lot of turnover and a hiring freeze. Since she'd been so effective previously, the Accounting group was practically begging her boss to send her back.

Later that day I received this text from her: "Ben, I think I can make this work for all of us."

When I talked to her, she explained that she'd agreed to help Accounting temporarily, but she'd asked in return for additional funds for her sales projects and to hire an outside team to help with her next sales event.

She just had to reframe the situation as a negotiation opportunity rather than another chance to "take one for the team." She could help Accounting, keep the job she loved, and negotiate for future assistance.

> Reframe the situation as a negotiation opportunity rather than another chance to "take one for the team."

Assume a Negotiation Perspective at Work

Based on my interactions with coworkers and clients, I believe that Susan's experience is typical. Employees don't assume a negotiation perspective at work, and that's a common reason for so much dissatisfaction. Daily life at the office can appear to be one surrender after another.

But most employees make two mistakes. First, they think of negotiation too narrowly, and secondly, they view it as disrespectful.

> But imagine your current job with the same salary but more flexibility or more alignment to the work that motivates you? That's what adopting a negotiation perspective can accomplish.

Many seem to think that money is the only negotiable, but in reality there's a much broader spectrum of conditions to negotiate, and many are much easier to negotiate than money or job title.

Negotiating for a raise or promotion can become very complicated because your boss and even your HR person may not be the final decision maker, and lots of restrictions like job bands and payment structures may limit their flexibility.

> In reality there's a much broader spectrum of conditions to negotiate, and many are much easier to negotiate than money or job title.

Most employees never consider negotiating about such conditions as setting boundaries for checking email or taking business calls at night or on vacation, or redefining work responsibilities, office location, start time, work from home, flex hours, their supervisor, or colleagues.

Making improvements in those areas are often a much smaller hill to climb than changing your salary or title and may lead you farther down the road toward sustaining the job you love.

The second mistake that employees often make is to believe that negotiating on their own behalf is somehow disrespectful to their boss or coworkers.

Negotiating is the ultimate sign of respect, however. It honors the person with whom you're negotiating, and it honors you, because the purpose is a mutually beneficial and satisfying outcome.

> Negotiating is the ultimate sign of respect

Here's a personal example, but it's one that comes up for a lot of employees.

Relocating to the City of Your Dreams Without Having to Quit

I'd been working on creating a job I could love for a while with my company, but I needed to make a change. I was ready to leave New York City to be closer to family and to start a family of our own.

I didn't want to give up the relationships, my role, or all the trust I'd established at my company, but I wanted to relocate to the city of my dreams: Charleston, South Carolina.

Sure, I could have looked for a new position in Charleston, but I wanted to stay with my company. I'd be putting a three-hour flight between me and the office where most of my coworkers were. Sure I could work remotely—but that's really remote.

The temptation in this situation was to make the move about me and my needs: walking into the boss's office and saying, "This work situation just isn't right for me."

Instead I adopted a negotiation mentality. I didn't lay down an ultimatum. I offered flexibility on timing, whether I worked from an office or home, and how often I'd travel to the home office.

The CPO's response? "Okay, Ben, but we're not paying for your relocation."

I walked out of there feeling like I'd won the lottery. I found myself more engaged, working harder than ever. I wanted to prove that this could work.

So I won the flexibility to live where I wanted and work where I wanted with zero disruption to my steady paycheck and seniority. Turns out that my new working arrangement led to my winning better results than ever for the company and my boss.

While this was a one-time major negotiation that worked out well for all parties, you don't have to wait for a big moment. In fact, it's better to bring a negotiation perspective to work every single day.

Bring a Negotiation Perspective to Work Every Day

Adopt a negotiation perspective when you walk in the office door each morning, along with these three strategies:

1. When you give, ask for a get.
2. Teach people how to treat you.
3. Practice saying "no" without guilt.

Approach #1: When you give, ask for a get.

When you're asked to give time, advice, or money, always consider the request you could make in return, even if you don't make it right then. All requests that people make, whether internal or external to your organization, can lead to an exchange of equal value.

For example, when someone asks for your help with a project outside the scope of your job, perhaps you drop everything and help. A nice gesture, but what happens to your priorities that are left undone and falling behind schedule?

> Start considering what an equal exchange of value could be whether or not you ask for it, just to get in the habit.

Consider a different, mutually beneficial script:

> "Sure I'll help, and will you please help me with my project later today so I can finish on time?"

or

> "Sure. Would you take a look at this beforehand and give me feedback? I'll be able to spend more time helping you then."

Perhaps you're asked to sacrifice personal time to complete a project. Instead of gutting it out and resenting it, bring the negotiation mindset:

> "I'd be happy to see this through, but since that means time after hours and on the weekend, I'd like an afternoon off next week."

or

> "Yes, and I'd like to take care of the work from home this week."

Although crucial to a healthy work environment, negotiation may not be effective at first in some organizations. People who are not accustomed to the negotiation perspective may bristle or say no when you ask for something in return. More about no in a minute, but realize that you have an option at that point: fulfill their request anyway, or offer an alternative "get."

In another situation, the boss or boss's boss delivers an urgent request. Asking for something in return in that high-pressure moment might jeopardize your job. My recommendation is to clarify and fulfill their request immediately, but mentally file your "give away" for a potential future "get." For example, I don't think the flight on the toilet seat paid for my MBA, but calling on that story later made me more memorable.

Notice which part of a request is simply doing your job, versus accomplishing something beyond its scope. Many employees spend most of their days fulfilling requests beyond the scope of their job, and this is the territory for negotiation.

The give and get approach works in the opposite direction, too. When you ask someone for help, offer an exchange of equal value. They'll be more likely to reciprocate in the future.

This leads to the next point.

Approach #2: Teach people how to treat you.

When I began my career, I believed that going above and beyond to fulfill everyone's requests was just doing my job. I didn't realize that by consistently saying yes to all requests from my boss and coworkers, it was guaranteed they'd keep asking and asking.

I'd unknowingly taught them to treat me like a request-filling machine who would keep giving without ever receiving a "get" beyond the paycheck. I was stretched too thin, and something had to change.

> I'd unknowingly taught them to treat me like a request-filling machine who would keep giving without ever receiving a "get" beyond the paycheck.

I finally understood that the job meant taking care of those core responsibilities; everything else was up for negotiation.

When I began to ask for help in return, I noticed an immediate slowdown in requests beyond the scope of my job. More importantly, I found people were willing to help if I clearly said what I wanted.

My habit became to ask for a "get" every time someone asked for a "give," and eventually, my coworkers started showing up with a "give" to offer. I'd effectively taught my coworkers, and even myself, how to treat each another. Everyone benefited.

Of course, there are situations at work where you don't want to give and you don't need a "get." You need to say no.

Approach #3: Say no without guilt.

I struggled with saying no for so long because it felt so uncomfortable. I didn't want to disappoint anyone, so saying yes seemed easier.

But this led to a lot of self-inflicted pain. I took on much more than I could do. I'd end up stressed out, burning the midnight oil, and predictably, dropping the ball and making things far worse for everyone involved.

I knew that saying no more often would free me to set priorities well and succeed more often. Knowing you should say no, and actually saying no, are very different, however.

> Never saying no = self-inflicted pain.

From the book, *Language and the Pursuit of Happiness*, by Chalmers Brothers, I learned to view saying no, not as "a rejection of the person," but as "a decline of their request."

> View saying no, not as "a rejection of the person," but as "a decline of their request."

This wisdom immediately lifted my guilt. It made saying no a lot less personal.

No one likes rejection, so from then on, whenever I delivered a no at work, I'd emphasize the request so the asker didn't hear it as a personal rejection. This may sound like semantics, but it makes a big difference.

Making the "no" specific to a request (or an offer) is the key to ensuring the other person receives it as a decline of a request rather than a rejection as a person.

Repeat the request, and then use the word "decline" or "no." Go one step farther with a counter offer.

For example:

> Instead of saying, "I'm not going to do that for you."

> Say, "I'm not doing that report this week, but how about if I complete it next Friday?"

Instead of saying, "I'm not going to work on your project this weekend."

Say, "I won't be working on your project this weekend, but what if you ask John?"

Avoid saying, "I'm sorry," because people see through that unless you're *really* sorry. Avoid saying, "Don't take this personally," because that makes it personal. Avoid saying, "I have to say no because of my boss," because that passes the buck—and they might call your bluff by talking to your boss, who might tell you to do it anyway.

Sometimes no matter how you frame that no, the other party will interpret it as a rejection.

Action: Recall the last time someone said no to you at work. Did you take it personally? What's it like to consider the no a decline of your request versus a rejection of you?

Lastly, saying no is a human right. The only people who risk their lives by saying no are enslaved, the victims of the most serious crime against humanity. If you ever catch yourself thinking, *I can't say no,* question that thought.

You're always choosing to say yes or no, even if you've said yes so often to your boss, coworkers, and spouse that it's become the *modus operandi* of your relationships. It's never too late to adopt a negotiation mindset, and say no.

Six Strategies for Saying No Without Getting Fired

The art of saying no is indispensable. It is not always easy, however, and in some circumstances it could jeopardize your employment.

Fortunately, there are many ways to decline a request without actually saying no.

Here are six ways to say no without saying no, along with scripts for each.

Strategy 1: The "Prioritizer" (highly effective with executive leadership and direct bosses but not clients or coworkers)

> Instead of no, say, "I'm working on _____, _____, and _____. How would this assignment rank on that list, in terms of priority?"

This strategy shows your willingness to help and enlists their support in setting priorities. Sometimes this leads the asker to take the request to someone else, freeing you to get back to work. Another benefit is that the asker might come up with someone to take care of another of your priorities to free you up to address this request.

Strategy 2: The "Booked" (highly effective with coworkers, but not bosses or clients)

> "I'm booked until _____. I can put it on my list and get to it then. Does that timing work for you?"

Again you're demonstrating your willingness to help, but also communicating that if the request is urgent, better to take it somewhere else because you are booked.

Strategy 3: The "Clarifier" (highly effective with everyone, including clients)

> "Please be more specific about _____."

> "What does completion of _____ look like?"

> "When do you need _____ by?" (You can follow this question with the Booked or Prioritizer strategy.)

Often, when someone shows up with a request, they're not entirely sure what they are asking for and what would satisfy their request. Asking them to clarify the details often transforms a huge task into a simple one, or they realize asking someone else makes more sense, or they answer their own question!

> Asking them to clarify the details often transforms a huge task into a simple one, or they realize asking someone else makes more sense, or they answer their own question!

Strategy 4: The "Breather" (helpful with everyone, including clients)

"I'll get back to you by _____."

"I'll check with my (boss, to-do list, team, spouse) and get back to you by _____."

This strategy is especially helpful with people who are pushing you to agree to their request on the spot. It creates a space for you to get perspective before agreeing. And it may be easier for you to say no by email later, than in the face-to-face situation where they may reject your no and keep pushing.

Strategy 5: The "Direct" (a strategy that depends on your confidence with the person to whom you're speaking)

"No" or "I decline."

A majorly bold move. One of the most direct ways to say no and therefore one of the most respectful. The challenge I find with saying no this way is that often people want an excuse or an explanation. If you offer any, the conversation could become tricky because they may not respect your reason. I recommend exploring other strategies before this one.

Strategy 6: The "Trade-Off" (also known as the "Negotiator," works well at all levels and also with customers)

"I will do _____ if you would gladly do _____."

One of my favorites, and under-utilized. Instead of saying no, you propose a trade-off, which may lead to negotiation and mutual satisfaction for both of you.

Dealing With an Unreasonable Boss Without Getting Into Trouble

Now, we'll turn to negotiating for what you want when faced with one of the most difficult challenges in any workplace: an unreasonable boss.

Pursuing what you want when working for an unreasonable boss is a challenge. No matter how hard you work, the unreasonable boss is never happy and always demanding more—a slippery slope toward burnout for you.

No matter how much past success you've had, you may begin to question your ability and find your confidence shaken. But if you can learn to thrive while working for an unreasonable boss, you'll be able to thrive anywhere.

Finding a Way to Work with an Unreasonable Boss

When I moved to Manhattan, I started off on the wrong foot with the boss, and things got worse fast. I put in long hours without results coming very quickly.

My boss began to come down on me about the lack of results, and directly questioned whether I was cut out for the job. He threatened to demote me and even lobbed insults about "the way they do business back in Alabama."

First, I pushed back, but then gradually I resorted to survival mode, going through the motions and staying out of his way. I approached HR but nothing seemed to happen. As the berating escalated, I called every recruiter I knew to find an escape.

I had to make a change, so while he was on a trip to Europe, I quietly lined up another job in the same company at an office across town. The evening before he returned from Europe, I packed up my office under cover of darkness. My office was vacant when he arrived the next day. I sealed the deal by sending him a "Dear John" email concerning my new position.

By the way, better not to deal with your boss with a "Dear John" email. He was furious, and our future interactions did not go well. My new boss offered me protection, but it was still incredibly awkward when our paths crossed.

> By the way, better not to deal with your boss with a "Dear John" email.

I pushed myself to the limit working for that unreasonable boss, but learned invaluable lessons that enabled me to thrive under the next unreasonable boss I encountered a few years later. And that second experience shaped my career.

Through experiences like these, you can become more self-reliant and creative in negotiating for what you want. Even though it's painful, you come out the other side wiser, more confident, and much smarter about what *not* to do.

3 Steps to Thrive While Working For an Unreasonable Boss

I learned these strategies the hard way.

Step #1: Clarify their interests first. In the heat of the moment, it is natural to start the conversation with what you want—but not effective. You'll come off sounding whiny and needy, and the response you get will often translate as "suck it up" or "you go figure it out."

> Expose their interests first, and address them.

Looking back, I never understood what motivated that boss or even the pressure he was under. Most employees assume that the boss will tell you, but that's a dangerous assumption because without that knowledge, you're flying blind.

Clarify your boss's concerns by finding out:

- Why does your boss work in the first place?
- What are his or her annual goals? How are these measured?
- Are you and the group performing to those goals?
- What pressures is the boss under?
- What is his relationship with his boss?

It may seem forward or out-of-the box to ask these questions directly, but answers will help you a lot. If you choose not to ask the boss directly, ask coworkers or the boss's peers.

This knowledge will help you craft conversations in a way that considers the boss's interests, along with yours.

Step #2: Learn to speak their language. The cold truth about conversations with the boss is that it doesn't matter what you say; it only matters what he or she hears.

> it doesn't matter what you say; it only matters what he or she hears

With that in mind, speak in a way that resonates. Notice when she speaks if she refers to dollars, headcount, savings, feelings, relationships, or hypothetical situations, and then consider incorporating similar examples when you speak with her.

Even if this strategy differs from your usual approach, it will ensure your words are heard. The boss will be more likely to listen and to understand. Looking back at my situation, I was talking processes and prospecting, and this only irritated the boss further. He wanted to talk about closing deals. Discussing that first might have enlisted his support.

Step #3: Be clear about what you want. Does the boss know what you want in your work day? Many employees never make this clear and leave the outcome up to chance.

The happiest employees articulate *in detail* what kind of job and work day would be ideal, and they share it with the boss. Of course, that doesn't mean everything falls into place immediately, but over time, this information becomes part of the decision making process about organizational changes and work load.

> The happiest employees articulate *in detail* what kind of job and work day would be ideal, and they share it with the boss.

Action: The ideal workday exercise. With a sheet of paper and a timer, brainstorm for 10 minutes what your ideal workday would look like. What work activities would fill your day? What time would you arrive and leave? With whom would you work? Take one or two nuggets from the brainstorm, and integrate them into your next conversation with your boss.

The Courage to Get Clear and Make the Ask

We'd spent weeks preparing for my client Janet's annual review. Although she'd been through 11 already, this one was different.

She'd had a banner year at work and decided that what she most wanted wasn't a raise or promotion, but a more flexible schedule. She wanted to work from home two days per week.

She wanted to ask to work part-time for a while so she could be at home more with her family. Originally, she had come to talk with me about planning her exit strategy, but now she wanted to figure out a way to stay. In our discussions, she realized how much experience and value she brought to the organization. She'd generated a lot of trust, strong relationships, and proof that she could get the job done. She figured she would work from home two days a week, become even more productive, and be at home when her children came home from school. She could use the occasional break to tidy up the house and actually cook dinner for her family.

She clarified her boss's interests first. She spent the time in advance anticipating what concerns her boss might have and what benefits the new situation might confer on her boss and coworkers. She knew her boss was under a lot of pressure to deliver big results the following year, and several of her projects were crucial to that goal, and so her project timelines couldn't slip.

In her annual review, she made her request to work from home and began by speaking her boss's language with her plans to ensure her projects would succeed on time. She explained how much more she could concentrate at home and how this time would contribute to the overall process. She also addressed how communication would occur on those days.

Then she was clear about what she wanted. Janet's boss agreed to one day at home per week for the first quarter and, if everything was running smoothly at that point, he'd consider adding a second day.

Although Janet had good annual reviews previously, she was most proud of this one because she'd had the courage to ask for what she wanted while addressing the concerns of her boss and company—truly a win–win–win strategy.

> She was most proud of this one because she'd had the courage to ask for what she wanted while addressing the concerns of her boss and company—truly a win-win-win strategy.

Now that we've covered negotiating for what you want without hurting the company, we'll talk about owning the packaging of your messages at work. Employees often find that the more effective their messaging, the less negotiating they have to do.

Chapter 9

OWN YOUR MESSAGE

Marketing is too important to be left to the marketing department.

David Packard, Co-Founder Hewlett-Packard

E ver considered why some messages you write or speak either:

- resonate and compel others to action, or
- create a misunderstanding or fall flat?

Owning your messages means taking responsibility for the outcome. It's not what you say, it's what people ultimately hear that often determines the success of your communication.

> Owning your messages means taking responsibility for the outcome.

Here's a personal example. We were in the final stage of a major contract, and going all in as an organization. The contract meant either a flood of new growth or a major loss of business. I was on the negotiation team and desperate for seven of our company locations across the U.S. to confirm whether they could deliver on the customer's demands.

We were in a crisis time crunch, so instead of telephoning I sent an email with this message in the subject line:

"Please Respond ASAP."

An hour passed. Only one location responded, probably because she was a friend of mine.

Everyone knew how important this was, and I couldn't believe the delay. In my anger, I sent another message with this headline:

"Your Job and Mine Could Be at Stake."

I received responses from all locations within minutes, and we confidently closed the deal.

In that moment, I understood the importance of owning my messaging.

Market to Your Boss, and Help Your Career

I struggled to write this chapter, because of my corporate roots. In organizational life, we don't market to each other well. We rely on job titles, authority, and sheer goodwill to persuade others to act.

These tactics can get the job done in the short term, but over time they lose their effectiveness. Escalating demands up the organization chart becomes a bit like the boy who cried wolf. Escalate too many times, and before long, people stop responding.

> Escalating demands up the organization chart becomes a bit like the boy who cried wolf. Escalate too many times, and before long, people stop responding.

Far more advantageous and empowering is to direct your marketing toward the boss and coworkers. Developing this skill gains you more influence and the capacity for a much greater impact within the organization.

Own the Effectiveness of Your Messages

Joseph explained that no one listened to him at the office. He's a leader in his field, and has been the resident expert for well over two decades. He's dedicated and truly cares about his company.

He knows what should be done to make things better, but no one seems to listen.

For years, he's been telling everyone how to fix things, but nothing's happened, and in many cases, they're heading in the wrong direction.

He's frustrated, burned out, and ready to hit the eject button. He'd pretty much given up making any difference in his current position and was contemplating moving to another company, although without high expectations.

Although Joseph's situation sounded bleak, we discovered something that worked for him. In place of the same old story of "I'm not being heard," he shifted to "I'm not getting my message across."

He began to think like a masterful marketer in how he framed the problems and solutions. This simple shift put him in control, and things began to change when he became the player, instead of the victim.

Imagine if everyone at the office began owning their own communication, and taking charge of who hears the message and how well it's understood.

Things would change!

The next time you find yourself feeling frustrated at the office, ask yourself, "How can I more effectively get my message across?"

"How can I more effectively get my message across?"

One Simple Marketing Question
That Reduces Anxiety

When I get stuck on a project or anxious about a big talk, I go back to that simple question: "How can I more effectively get my message across?"

Just reflecting on it calms me, reminds me why I do this work, and propels me forward.

Answering this question takes your thoughts instantly away from your ego and back to your capacity to help others. It's like standing on stage and shifting the spotlight back onto the crowd. You relax, and you're able to compose a more effective message to reach the intended audience.

Action: Apply this question when planning the introduction to your next meeting. Write out the question, along with a few ideas in response, addressing how the meeting serves the attendees. Share these ideas with them when you kick things off. Notice how much the message you've crafted resonates. Note: If you can't think of any ways that the meeting serves the audience, consider canceling it.

How to Market to Your Boss and Coworkers
to Get What You Want

To craft even more effective messages for the boss and coworkers, employ these three additional marketing strategies:

- **Meet them where they are.** Consider the audience before writing an email, leading a call, or presenting, or your message may fall flat. Can your message address a problem they're currently facing? This is critical, especially in creating an email subject line or

> How does your message address a problem they're currently facing?

presentation title. Otherwise, you'll lose your reader and your audience before you begin.

- **Lead with WIFM.** It's incredibly helpful to assume that the audience is always wondering, "What's in it for me?" (Tagged WIFM in marketing circles.) Instead of making them guess, offer the answer upfront to build engagement and interest, no later than the third sentence of any conference call or presentation. And include the answer in the reference line of all emails. You'll probably notice an immediate difference in the responses you get. "Please Respond ASAP" had no WIFM. "Your Job and Mine could be at Stake" put it out there directly and won a much quicker and complete response.

> "What's in it for me?"

- **Prioritize the call to action.** I read a lot of emails and sit through presentations and conference calls that do not present a clear next step or even ask people to do anything. For better results, begin your next email or meeting by asking yourself what you want people to do afterwards, and work backwards from there.

> Begin your next email or meeting by asking yourself what you want people to do.

Action: Open your email and look at the last three emails you've sent. Do these messages meet them where they are, lead with WIFM, and include a clear call to action? If not, consider resending and notice any difference in the responses.

Pay For Your MBA With OPM

When I first thought about asking my company to pay for my MBA, I thought about it as a negotiation. Remarkably, the success I had was more about how I owned my message and identified it as a marketing opportunity.

> Sometimes packaging your message well means avoiding the need for negotiation altogether, even when you're asking for something big.

My organization had never paid for anyone's MBA before, and attending classes would limit my travel schedule. I was prepared to make significant concessions with my job and even my salary, but I never had to go there.

The end result was the organization agreed to pay most of the MBA costs and to support my taking time off to attend class and team projects. I continued to deliver results at work while I went to school. I had a great experience and even laid the groundwork for my coworkers to do the same.

Here's how I applied these marketing strategies to get the results I wanted:

- **Meet them where they are.** Before I made this request, I thought about it from my boss's perspective. What would his concerns be? Who would he have to persuade? What experience did he have with this type of request? What would be most important to him? I knew their primary concern would be whether I could maintain my current workload and deliver a return on their investment in the MBA. I made sure to address those points when I presented the idea.
- **Lead with WIFM.** I imagined that my boss was sitting there thinking "what's in it for me," so I led with WIFM, despite the temptation to start my presentation with how important it was to me to obtain an MBA. I led with the

benefits for the boss and the organization, and I never mentioned how it would benefit my career (although they probably understood that). I did my research to understand the curriculum and talked to alumni of the program. It was easy then to link the MBA to enabling me to contribute more and make a bigger impact in my current role. I even pointed out school projects from the curriculum that I could complete in a dual capacity to deliver savings for our organization.

- **Prioritize the call to action.** Although we reached a verbal agreement by the end of the meeting, the details were still fuzzy. I anticipated this result, so I drafted a letter of support in advance that only required a signature and to write in the amount they would contribute. At the end of the conversation, I made the call-to-action very simple: I pulled out the letter and asked my boss to sign. We hadn't figured out all the logistics of making the payment, but I walked out of the office with an agreement in writing. I felt great, and he did too.

Now that we've covered sustaining the job you love through negotiating on your own behalf and owning your message, it's time to make your work day easier by bringing a personal side to the office.

Chapter 10

BRING YOUR PERSONAL SIDE TO WORK

Balance suggests a perfect equilibrium. There is no such thing.
That is a false expectation....There are going to be priorities and
dimensions of your life; how you integrate them is how you
find true happiness.

Denise Morisson, CEO, Campbell Soup

To sustain the job you love, it's important to consider how you can show up energized and authentic, without having to fake it. Sure you can fake a smile and enthusiasm for a while, but eventually it becomes too exhausting.

One of the best tips for sustaining the job you love is to start to integrate your work and personal life. Think of your life in both realms as a big puzzle, and you're the one at the helm on the lookout for ways to fit these pieces together. It can be something as simple as moving your staff meetings to a more interesting location or going around the room and finding out how everyone's weekend was before diving into the day's business.

> Just by bringing a personal side to the office, you'll find the job you love becomes even better.

Become Energized and Authentic Without Selling Your Soul

I was freaking out. I'd been blogging under a secret identity while still in my corporate job. Now I was publishing my first article as "Ben Fanning" and sharing it on my company's private LinkedIn group.

Until that moment, I'd kept my passion separate from my day job. I lost a lot of sleep that night, because I was nervous and because I was energized by sharing this personal side of myself with my coworkers.

The next day, no one at the office mentioned the article I'd shared. It was business as usual.

But when I got home, I found the article had generated hundreds of views. Apparently, no one was comfortable mentioning it to me directly at work, but I could see they'd read it.

I continued to post articles each week and, gradually, as weeks passed, people began to mention how they appreciated my perspective. That's when I understood the importance of sharing this side of myself with my coworkers.

Many of my clients have benefited from this perspective. They report that taking the step toward work-life integration improved their motivation and relationships at work. One client started a lunch-and-learn program to share her passion for cooking with her coworkers. She prepared busy mom/dad recipe cards and food samples to share. Now other employees are bringing recipes to exchange, too.

Another employee started a monthly book club coffee to talk about books on leadership or career development, scheduled before the work day began. Another client passionate about fitness led a weight-loss challenge and got the company to sponsor the program.

How to Bring Yourself to the Office

I discovered incredible benefits when I brought all of Ben to the office: the gentle Ben who interacts with his baby, the confident Ben who smashes a forehand on the tennis court, and the relaxed Ben from yoga class. Tackling difficult conversations and challenges all became much easier when I brought myself to the work. Best of all, I felt far less tired at the end of the work week.

> Tackling difficult conversations and challenges all became much easier when I brought myself to the work.

Action: Sometimes a little momentum is enough to get started:

1. Think about that person at work with whom you're having difficulty.
2. Consider whether you're bringing your whole self to that conversation.
3. What else could you bring to that conversation? Attentiveness, passion, fun, humor, creativity?
4. When that little voice in your head says, "That won't work for me at the office," stop and ask, "Why not?"
5. Notice what happens.

After practicing, you'll discover that you're more effective and your day has more joy and more mojo.

Warning: This Might be Fun

Many of my clients are surprised to discover how much fun bringing your personal side to work can be.

- The consultant who discovers that his love of fly-fishing actually makes him more peaceful and mindful during this work day:
  Richard started by placing fly-fishing photos in his office and on his screen saver to ease his mind when returning to his office after

a difficult meeting. Showing this side of himself also helped his coworkers and direct reports connect with him in a different way.

- The marketing executive who discovers how her passion for cooking helps her develop deeper relationships at work that are more trusting:
  Eve is a full-time working mom, passionate about preparing healthy food for her children despite her busy schedule. Instead of just attending another business lunch or happy hour, she shared her tips and recipes with her coworkers.

- The sales manager who finds that her love of improv and acting can make sales calls much more exciting and engaging:
  Kara was sick of the no's that she and her sales team faced daily. Every time she walked in the office, she felt like she was "checking her soul at the door." She had a mantra: "Focus on results." Although she got results, she felt she was doing so at the expense of her team's morale and her sanity. Outside of work, she was light-hearted and playful, enjoying live music and performing improv, but she didn't see how this side of herself fit in the workplace. She left her joyful side outside. In our work together, she experimented with bringing the fun-loving side of herself to work and discovered that doing so helped keep her and her team motivated and reduced stress when things got heated.

> Blurring the lines between personal and professional can make your work day more authentic, more fun, and more motivating

Action: The "How was Your Weekend" test. One of the easiest ways to bring a personal side to work is to share a little bit about your life outside of work, and then ask someone else the question. Evaluate your beliefs and your comfort in bringing a personal side to work by asking this question.

Now, the ultimate step to sustain the job you love is to create the work environment to help you maintain your motivation.

Chapter 11

REVITALIZE A DEAD OFFICE INTO AN INSPIRING PLACE TO WORK

How was your day? If your answer was "fine,"
then I don't think you were leading.

Seth Godin, *Tribes*

One of the best ways to sustain the job you love is to create an office environment that provides an inspiring, supportive atmosphere.

But when was the last time you felt an emotional connection at the office? One that led to working with a deeper sense of connection and purpose?

> When you create an emotional connection at the office, you make it a more enjoyable place to work, boost morale, and even improve communication.

You can do this by learning to "put your mouth where your heart is," which often triggers a ripple effect that goes beyond one conversation and may influence the entire organization.

Our Office Needed to Revitalize

Working in a "dead" office was one of the hardest things I've ever done.

I'd previously worked in a place where the office was like family. It was full of camaraderie, engagement, and even the occasional practical joke.

I'd invited the office to my wedding 4.5 hours away—and most of them came.

But the office I'd worked in the last several years had become a like a morgue.

The silence was so deafening it was creepy. People frequently spoke in a whisper and usually kept their office doors shut.

Their faces were set in a look of discomfort and stress and some even resembled the "working dead," physically showing up to work but checking their hearts and passions at the door. They seemed disconnected from their work and from one another. Many employees didn't even know the person in the office next door, not to mention all those who worked in different buildings or remotely.

I started noticing a sinking feeling in the pit of my stomach whenever I pulled into the parking lot.

It seemed like a problem too big to tackle.

I never expected that it would start with one personal interaction.

When the Corporate Mask Comes Off

"Ben, my son was just seriously wounded in Afghanistan. He might lose both legs."

(pause)

That was how the phone conversation started with Kevin, who'd been my coworker for years. I realized in that moment that we'd always kept it light, and this news hit me like a ton of bricks. I was tempted to offer my sympathy and then return our discussion to "the numbers," but I couldn't.

We sat in silence. Then I asked, "How are you doing?"

That's when the corporate mask came off, and we had our first real conversation. I learned about his relationship with his son, and how his wife was coping with this new challenge. He shared his concerns about his son's future, and even the disturbing dreams he was having. For some reason, I shared my fears about becoming the father I wanted to be.

> That conversation only took 15 minutes, but it transformed our relationship from that day onwards.

The Ripple Effect – How One Conversation Ends a War at Work

Kevin and I worked in different offices, and we'd rarely seen each other in person. Yet, I was amazed by the ripple effect of that one phone conversation.

We suddenly had an emotional connection that influenced our subsequent interactions. I immediately noticed how it affected our daily work as we became much more intentional with our communication.

We stopped lobbing problems back-and-forth, and much of the combative behavior that had showed up as we defended our territories transformed into gentleness, helpfulness, and trust.

We began to check in periodically to keep informed on what was happening in our respective areas. The biggest surprise, though, was our new patience with each other.

Kevin has a technical background and would take the time to explain details to me, and I reciprocated by explaining the deals I was negotiating and how each might influence his area.

And that was only the first ripple.

The Second Ripple – The Taboo Staff Meeting Topic

The next ripple occurred in one of our larger staff meetings and permanently changed their tone.

Instead of opening the call with work frustrations, Kevin and I spontaneously struck up a conversation and shared a bit of our personal lives. Others listening began to yearn to be part of the deeper conversation and share something of themselves.

Recognize that we had never talked about our families before on these calls.

At first, this happened out of concern for Kevin's son, but over time we held the space open for this interaction. Talking together this way connected everyone and resulted in a fully present and attentive group, improving our connection as a team, our work environment, and our results.

> Talking together this way connected everyone and resulted in a fully present and attentive group, improving our connection as a team, our work environment, and our results.

The Third Ripple and Beyond – Tackling a Crisis by Humanizing Your Coworkers

The next ripple occurred in the context of how each team member approached cross-functional projects. One area of the budget was out of control and bleeding money. We were all under immense pressure to find the root cause and resolve it as quickly as possible.

This purpose was complicated by the size and complexity of the team (employees from nine different divisions of the organization). Normally, we'd schedule a conference call, demand everyone attend, and jump into the issue.

The problem was that we frequently didn't know half the people in the meeting. We'd identify people by their category, like this: "Is anyone from Order Management on the call? Is anyone from Shipping on the call?"

Cold and impersonal.

We were so intent on getting the work done that we defaulted to treating people as interchangeable resources. The consequence was that it was easy to dehumanize our coworkers, assign blame, and avoid collaboration.

But we consciously decided to take a different approach.

The ripple from our previous conversations generated a new possibility. We opened our first call with the intention of recognizing everyone, and we clarified our expectations for the team. We explained that we wanted this project to work differently than it had before.

We asked everyone to identify themselves by name and the one achievement at the company of which they were most proud.

This rippled throughout the project. We'd show up intent on creating positive interactions, establishing better relationships across our organization, and successfully tackling one of the biggest cross-functional projects in which the team had ever been involved.

The project succeeded, and team members went on to drive other important projects. Many of these relationships are helpful to this day.

When I encounter these people in the halls, we still talk about the amazing work we did and how it changed our relationships with coworkers.

> We ultimately established the foundation for success by starting with the human side of business

The Wall That Stops You From a Bigger Impact at the Office

I'm convinced that when Kevin brought up his son's injury and we talked, that conversation set off a powerful ripple.

Why isn't everybody doing this?

The ripple never happened in the hundreds of previous conversations we'd had because we always had a wall between us.

This wall isn't all bad. It can protect, but it also inhibits productive conversations. Kevin and I were investing a lot of energy maintaining this wall. I could hear his voice, but I couldn't "see" him, and he couldn't "see" me.

It felt risky to bring our personal and emotional identities to work, and we were cozy and content on our side of the wall.

Bringing the Part of You That's Expert in Connecting

So what differentiates the daily interactions at work from interactions that have a ripple effect?

When you have a conversation that ripples, you have climbed over the wall to stand beside the other person.

When there's no wall and no hiding, you're vulnerable, and suddenly emotions and mood are front and center. When that happens, you've brought the side of yourself to the conversation that's expert in connecting.

That's what distinguishes conversations that ripple.

No Going Back

What is it about the moments that transform your relationship with someone and then ripple outward to others?

Your relationship has moved into a different space, and once you're over the wall, there's no going back.

There's no work and life, but work-life. Daily meetings become a place of connection as well as work.

> Every interaction becomes an opportunity for connection.

The labels disappear, and you'll notice that you are working together more effectively.

The ripple not only affects you and your interactions, but begins to send a ripple through the entire organization.

It can revitalize a dead office into an inspiring place to work.

3 Steps to Starting Your Own Ripple

To create your own ripple, climb over the wall between you and your coworkers.

Start with these 3 steps:

- **Listen:** When passing a coworker, listen to the voice in your head saying, "Something's going on here." Stop, instead of walking by. Ask the open-ended question, "What's going on with you today?" Then give that person your full, undivided attention. Sometimes the other person isn't ready to climb over the wall. If this is the case, just say, "I'm here if you'd like to talk." In my story, this happened when I stopped talking.

- **Allow**: Climbing over the wall is often uncomfortable and downright awkward. And yes, there's risk. Be brave enough to let the conversation happen. It requires bravery to start the conversation and to hold the space to allow it to happen. Instead of changing the topic to something lighter, I held the space for Kevin and encouraged him to talk to me. Then the conversation unfolded.
- **Reciprocate**: Reciprocate with your own vulnerability. Get down to the level where something's really at stake. Tap into your fears and offer them in return. When Kevin shared his fears, I didn't try to comfort him or solve his problem. I responded with my own.

You Can Make Your Office a More Inspiring Place to Work

You don't have to wait to start a positive ripple at your office.

Notice how these three simple steps start a ripple effect from your conversations at work. Instead of putting your money where your mouth is, try putting your mouth where your heart is.

Time to Get Creative

Creating the job you love is a journey. The good news is that you don't have to find it—you have the power to create it right where you are today.

Pick any of the ideas in this book, and share it with one of your coworkers, friends, or family to make your work day a more inspiring experience.

Here they are in summary:

Step 1: Engage With the Potential of Your Current Job

- Prioritize creating the job you love over finding another one
- Redefine your beliefs about work
- Turn your work day into something to look forward to

Step 2: Cultivate the Work That Inspires You

- Unlock your internal motivation by starting with "why"
- Discover the work that motivates you
- Campaign for the work you love

Step 3: Create and Sustain the Job You Love

- Negotiate without others losing
- Own your messages
- Bring your personal side to work and inspire others

Last, don't forget to spend some time on the companion website for this book. You'll find templates, links to resources, additional content, interviews with employees who have transformed their jobs—all in the name of creating the job they love without quitting, and much, much more.

And for up-to-date information on creating the job you love, head over to my regularly updated blog at benfanning.com/quit.

5 Reasons Why I'm Your Ideal Guide for Your Career Transformation

1) You get support directly from the Chief Burnout Officer.
Everyone needs someone in their corner. I help professionals create the job they love without quitting, while continuing to work within a Fortune 100 company, keeping my finger on the pulse of challenges within organizations.

"The Zen Master of Career & Stress Management. Having worked with Ben and followed his practice, this book is a great study for anyone looking to merge their work-life balance while continuing to advance career goals."
–Mark Albright, **Vice President Sports Authority**

2) You're in this with someone who has been there. I burned out in my career and almost quit my job. I was frustrated from years of unfulfilled expectations and career dreams. After getting discouraged, I finally raised my eyes from the treadmill and began showing up at work like a leader on my own terms. Just like you, I'm on the front lines and in the professional trenches at the office.

I was able to reignite my career. Then, after my own transformational experience, I noticed so many others showing up to work burned out, "sleep working" through their days, scared about losing their job, and too scared to do anything about it.

I realized I could help them.

> To support you on your own inspired path, sign-up for my weekly newsletter, which is chock full of tips and strategies to inspire your work day. Subscribe by signing up here: benfanning.com/quit

3) This isn't theory–you get a blueprint to guide you step by step. My process has made an impact in Forbes, SmartBrief, and Lifehack, and has been delivered on stage at conferences, company meetings, and even for the U.S. Bureau of Counterterrorism.

4) You get real world wisdom backed by dozens of case studies. I draw from my experience working for 16 years in companies such as Honeywell, The Sports Authority, DHL, and Russell Athletic.

"Working together has never seemed like "work" to me, but rather a fun conversation or exercise that I would compare to a good workout in the gym. Overall, working with Ben makes you feel better, improves work performance, and even improves your health."
–Andrew Hirsekorn, **McKinsey Consultant, Wharton Graduate**

5) You get someone qualified to help and entertain. You get more than mere academic qualifications. I'm a certified coach through the International Coach Federation with an undergraduate degree from the University of Alabama and an MBA from Georgia Tech. I've also trained in improv and storytelling and always infuse a dose of humor with motivation.

I'm passionate about sharing my experiences and teaching groups.

To discuss bulk book purchase incentives and check my availability for speaking at your next event or workshop, go to benfanning. com/speaker or email me at: Ben@BenFanning.com.

Acknowledgements

Thank you to everyone that's helped make the idea for this book a reality. I would like to extend particular gratitude to my key supporters on this project:

My wife for her unwavering support; my editor, Anne Poliakoff for her patience and persistence; my personal coach and marketing advisor David Koons (www.linkedin.com/in/davidkoons). My publisher, Chris O'Byrne and team at JETLAUNCH.

NYT Bestselling author and friend, Chris Brogan, for his insightful feedback and lessons in letting "Ben" emerge in the writing.

Bestselling author, Pam Slim for encouraging me think bigger in terms of how this book can make an impact the world especially within larger organizations.

Scott Dinsmore at Live Your Legend, for his ongoing support and helping me establish an inspiring community that has supported me from manuscript through launch.

Jonathan Mead, for his early feedback on brainstorming ideas that inspire.

Dan Newby, for helping me keep going to finish,

Then to all the corporate leaders who have supported me a long the way especially Brian Simons, Randy Dohne, Jerry Biegler, Gary Adams, Chris Cadigan, and Mark Albright.

And finally, to anyone who has been a client, subscribed to my newsletter, left a blog comment, seen me speak live, shared my writing with others, or emailed me to ask a question about how to create the job you love—thank you! You inspire me every day and continue to keep me on my game.

CPSIA information can be obtained at www.ICGtesting.com
Printed in the USA
LVOW05*0728191114

414480LV00001B/2/P

9 781941 142608